SOPHOCLES · I

Oedipus the King
Oedipus at Colonus
Antigone

THE COMPLETE GREEK TRAGEDIES

Edited by David Grene and Richmond Lattimore

SOPHOCLES · I

OEDIPUS THE KING

OEDIPUS AT COLONUS

ANTIGONE

*Translated
and with an Introduction by*
DAVID GRENE

Second Edition

THE UNIVERSITY OF CHICAGO PRESS

CHICAGO & LONDON

The University of Chicago Press, Chicago 60637
The University of Chicago Press, Ltd., London

Second edition published 1991 by
  The University of Chicago Press
Printed in the United States of America

11 10 09 08 07 06 05 04 03 02   9 10 11 12 13

Library of Congress Cataloging-in-Publication Data

Sophocles.
  [Works. English. 1991]
  Sophocles / translated and with an introduction by David
Grene. — 2nd ed.
     p.   cm. — (The Complete Greek tragedies)
  Contents: I. Oedipus the King — Oedipus at Colonus —
Antigone.
  ISBN 0-226-30792-1 (v. 1)
  1. Sophocles—Translations, English. 2. Greek drama
(Tragedy) —Translations into English. 3. Mythology, Greek—
Drama. I. Grene, David. II. Title. III. Series.
PA4414.A1G7   1991
882'.01—dc20   90-26350
                                                        CIP

⊗ The paper used in this publication meets the minimum
requirements of the American National Standard for Information
Sciences—Permanence of Paper for Printed Library Materials,
ANSI Z39.48-1992.

TABLE OF CONTENTS

PUBLISHER'S NOTE

In this edition of *Sophocles I* new translations by David Grene replace Robert Fitzgerald's translation of *Oedipus at Colonus* (1941) and Elizabeth Wyckoff's translation of *Antigone* (1954).

The complete collection of Greek tragedies edited by David Grene and Richmond Lattimore is available in nine paperback volumes. These are listed at the end of this volume.

INTRODUCTION

"The Theban Plays" by Sophocles

THIS series of plays, *Oedipus the King*, *Oedipus at Colonus*, and *Antigone*, was written over a wide interval of years. The dating is only approximate, for reliable evidence is lacking; but the *Antigone* was produced in 441 B.C. when Sophocles was probably fifty-four, and *Oedipus the King* some fourteen or fifteen years later. *Oedipus at Colonus* was apparently produced the year after its author's death at the age of ninety in 405 B.C. Thus, although the three plays are concerned with the same legend, they were not conceived and executed at the same time and with a single purpose, as is the case with Aeschylus' *Oresteia*. We can here see how a story teased the imagination of Sophocles until it found its final expression. We can see the degrees of variation in treatment he gave the myth each time he handled it. And perhaps we can come to some notion of what the myths meant to Sophocles as raw material for the theater.

The internal dramatic dates of the three plays do not agree with the order of their composition. As far as the legend is concerned, the story runs in sequence: *Oedipus the King*, *Oedipus at Colonus*, *Antigone*. But Sophocles wrote them in the order: *Antigone*, *Oedipus the King*, *Oedipus at Colonus*. In view of this and the long interval between the composition of the individual plays, we would expect some inconsistencies between the three versions. And there are fairly serious inconsistencies—in facts, for instance. At the conclusion of *Oedipus the King*, Creon is in undisputed authority after the removal of Oedipus. Though he appeals to him to look after his daughters, Oedipus refrains from asking Creon to do anything for his sons, who, he says, will be all right on their own (*OK* 1460). It is Creon who will succeed Oedipus in Thebes, and there is no question of any legitimate claim of Oedipus' descendants (*OK* 1418). But in *Antigone,* Creon tells the chorus that he has favorably observed their loyalty first to Oedipus and then to his sons, and so has hope of their devotion to himself. In *Oedipus at Colonus*—the last of the three plays he wrote—Sophocles makes one of his very few clumsy efforts to patch the discrepancies together. In *Oedipus at Colonus* (ll. 367 ff.), Ismene says that *at first* the two sons were willing to leave the throne to Creon in view of their fatal family heritage, but after a while they decided to take over the monarchy and the quarrel was only between themselves as to who should succeed. At this point Creon has vanished out of the picture altogether! Again, the responsibility for the decision to expel Oedipus from Thebes and keep him out rests, in *Oedipus the King,* entirely with Creon, who announces that he will consult Apollo in the matter. In *Oedipus at Colonus* his sons' guilt in condemning their father to exile is one of the bitterest counts in Oedipus' indictment of them (*OC* 1360 ff.). These are important differences. We do not know anything really certain about the manner of publication of the plays after their production. We know even less about Sophocles' treatment of his own scripts. Maybe he simply did not bother to keep them after he saw them as far as the stage, though that seems unlikely. Or it is possible and likelier that Sophocles, as he wrote the last play in extreme old age and in what seems to be the characteristic self-absorption of the last years of his life, cared little about whether *Oedipus at Colonus* exactly tallied, in its presentation, with the stories he had written thirty-seven and twenty-two years earlier.

Let us for the moment disregard the details of the story and concentrate on what would seem to be the central theme of the first two plays in order of composition. And here we find something very curious. Most critics have felt the significance of the *Antigone* to lie in the opposition of Creon and Antigone and all that this opposition represents. It is thus a play about something quite different from *Oedipus the King.* And yet what a remarkable similarity there is in the dilemma of Creon in *Antigone* and Oedipus himself in the first Oedipus play. In both of them a king has taken a decision which is disobeyed or questioned by his subjects. In both, the ruler misconstrues the role of the rebel and his own as a sovereign. In both, he has a crucial encounter with the priest Teiresias, who warns him that the forces of religion are against him. In both, he charges that the priest has been suborned. There the resemblance ends; for, after abusing the old prophet, Creon is overcome with fear of his authority and, too late, tries to undo his mistake. In *Oedipus the King* the king defies all assaults upon his decision until the deadly self-knowledge which starts to work in him has accomplished its course and he is convicted out of his own mouth.

Usually, as we know, the *Antigone* is interpreted entirely as the conflict between Creon and Antigone. It has often been regarded as the classical statement of the struggle between the law of the individual conscience and the central power of the state. Unquestionably, these issues are inherent in the play. Unquestionably, even, Sophocles would understand the modern way of seeing his play, for the issue of the opposition of the individual and the state was sufficiently present to his mind to make this significant for him. But can the parallelism between the position of Oedipus in the one play and Creon in the other be quite irrelevant to the interpretation of the two? And is it not very striking that such a large share of the *Antigone* should be devoted to the conclusion of the conflict, as far as Creon is concerned, and to the destruction of his human happiness?

What I would suggest is this: that Sophocles had at the time of writing the first play (in 442 B.C.) a theme in mind which centered in the Theban trilogy. One might express it by saying that it is the story of a ruler who makes a mistaken decision, though in good faith, and who then finds himself opposed in a fashion which he misunderstands and which induces him to persist in his mistake. This story is later on going to be that of a man who breaks divine law without realizing that he is doing so, and whose destruction is then brought about by the voice of the divine law in society. Between the *Antigone* and *Oedipus the King,* the theme has developed further, for in the latter play Sophocles is showing how the ruler who breaks the divine law may, for all he can see and understand, be entirely innocent, but nonetheless his guilt is an objective fact. In the third play, *Oedipus at Colonus,* this issue reaches its final statement. The old Oedipus is admittedly a kind of monster. Wherever he comes, people shrink from him. Yet his guilt carries with it some sort of innocence on which God will set his seal. For the old man is both cursed and blessed. The god gives him an extraordinary end, and the last place of his mortal habitation is blessed forever.

What this interpretation would mean, if correct, is that Sophocles started to write about the Theban legend, the story of Oedipus and his children, without having fully understood what he wanted to say about it. He may have been, and probably was, drawn, unknown to himself, to the dramatization of this particular legend because in it lay the material of the greatest theme of his later artistic life. But first he tried his hand at it in the opposition of Creon and Antigone. However, even while he did this, the character of Creon and his role in the play were shaping what was to be the decisive turn in the story he was going to write—the Oedipus saga.

Thus there is a certain elasticity in the entire treatment of myth. The author will accent a certain character at one time to suit a play and change the accent to suit another. Or he may even discover the same theme in a different myth. This is suggested by a short comparison of the *Philoctetes* and *Oedipus at Colonus,* both written in the last few years of Sophocles' life. The figure of Philoctetes, though occurring in a totally different legend from Oedipus, is a twin child with Oedipus in Sophocles' dramatic imagination. In both these plays, the *Philoctetes* and *Oedipus at Colonus,* the hero is a man whose value is inextricably coupled with his offensive quality. Philoctetes is the archer whose bow will overcome Troy. He is also the creature whose stinking infested wound moves everyone to disgust who has to do with him. Oedipus is accursed in the sight of all men; he had committed the two crimes, parricide and incest, which rendered him an outcast in any human society. But he is also the one to whom, at his end, God will give the marks of his favor, and the place where he is last seen on earth will be lucky and blessed. This combination of the evil and the good is too marked, in these two plays, to be accidental. It is surely the idea which inspired the old Sophocles for his two last plays. There is, however, an important further development of the theme in the *Oedipus at Colonus.* For there in Oedipus' mind the rational innocence—the fact that he had committed the offenses unknowingly—is, for him at least, important in God's final justification of him. Sophocles is declaring that the sin of Oedipus is real; that the consequences in the form of the loneliness, neglect, and suffering of the years of wandering are inevitable; but that the will and the consciousness are also some measure of man's sin—and when the sinner sinned necessarily and unwittingly, his suffering can be compensation enough for his guilt. He may at the end be blessed and a blessing. This is not the same doctrine as that of Aeschylus, when he asserts that through suffering comes wisdom. Nor is it the Christian doctrine of a man purified by suffering as by fire. Oedipus in his contact with Creon, in his interview with Polyneices shows himself as bitter, sudden in anger, and implacable as ever. He is indeed a monstrous old man. But at the last, he is, in a measure, *vindicated*. Yet in *Philoctetes* the theme of the union of the offensive and the beneficial, which in *Oedipus at Colonus* becomes the curse and the blessing, is seen without the addition of conscious innocence and unconscious guilt. Can we say that Sophocles finally felt that the consciousness of innocence in Oedipus is the balancing factor in the story? That in this sense *Oedipus at Colonus* is the further step beyond *Philoctetes* in the clarification of the dramatic subject which occupied the very old author? Or that the consciousness of innocence when linked with objective guilt is only the human shield against the cruelty of the irrational—that Oedipus is meaningful in his combination of guilt and innocence as a manifestation of God and of destiny and that his explanation of his conscious innocence is only the poor human inadequate explanation? Everyone will answer this according to his own choice. But, clearly, the theme of Philoctetes and the theme of the old Oedipus are connected.

If an analysis such as this has importance, it is to show the relation of Sophocles to the raw material of his plays—the myth. It is to show the maturing of a theme in Sophocles' mind and his successive treatments of it in the same and different legends. In the Oedipus story it is a certain fundamental situation which becomes significant for Sophocles, and the characters are altered to suit the story. Creon in the first, Oedipus in the second, are examples of the same sort of dilemma, even though the dilemma of Creon in the *Antigone* is incidental to the main emphasis of the play, which is on Antigone. But the dilemma was to be much more fruitful for Sophocles as a writer and thinker than the plain issue between Antigone and Creon. The dilemma resolves itself in the last play at the end of Sophocles' life into the dramatic statement of a principle, of the union of the blessed and the cursed, of the just and the unjust, and sometimes (not always) of the consciously innocent and the unconsciously guilty. The fact that Sophocles could in two successive treatments of the play fifteen years apart switch the parts of Creon and Oedipus indicates that neither the moral color of the characters nor even their identity was absolutely fixed in his mind. The same conclusion is borne out by the great similarity between the *Philoctetes* and the *Oedipus at Colonus*. Sophocles in his last days was incessantly thinking of the man who is blessed and cursed. For the theater he became once the lame castaway Philoctetes, who yet, in virtue of his archery, is to be the conqueror of Troy; in the next play he is Oedipus, who sinned against the order of human society but is still to be the blessing of Athens and the patron saint of Colonus. It is the theme and not the man that matters. Consequently, it is the kernel of the legend, as he saw it for the moment, that is sacred for Sophocles, not the identification of all the characters in a certain relation to one another. True, he has treated the Oedipus story three times in his life, which means that the Oedipus story had a certain fascination for him—that somehow hidden in it he knew there was what he wanted to say. But he did not have to think of the whole story and the interdependence of its characters when he made his changes each time. One stage of the theme borne by the hero is given to a character in a totally different myth. The sequence is Creon, Oedipus, Philoctetes, Oedipus. It may seem absurd to link Creon, the obvious form of tyrant (as conceived by the Athenians), and Philoctetes. But it is the progression we should notice. The tyrant who with true and good intentions orders what is wrong, morally and religiously, is crudely represented in Creon; he is much more subtly represented in Oedipus himself in the next play. But the similarity of the situation and the nature of the opposition to him proves how generically the character is conceived. You can switch the labels, and Creon becomes Oedipus. But if the character is generic, the situation is deepening. We are beginning to understand *why* a certain sort of tyrant may be a tyrant and in a shadowy way how conscious and unconscious guilt are related. In the *Philoctetes* and *Oedipus at Colonus* the situation is being seen in its last stages. We are no longer concerned with how Philoctetes came to sin or how Oedipus is the author of his own ruin. But only how does it feel to be an object both of disgust and of fear to your fellows, while you yourself are simultaneously aware of the injustice of your treatment and at last, in *Oedipus at Colonus,* of the objective proofs of God's favor.

For Sophocles the myth was the treatment of the generic aspect of human dilemmas. What he made of the myth in his plays was neither history nor the kind of dramatic creation represented by *Hamlet* or *Macbeth*. Not history, for in no sense is the uniqueness of the event or the uniqueness of the character important; not drama in the Shakespearean sense, because Sophocles' figures do not have, as Shakespeare's do, the timeless and complete reality in themselves. Behind the figure of Oedipus or Creon stands the tyrant of the legend; and behind the tyrant of the legend, the meaning of all despotic authority. Behind the old Oedipus is the beggar and wanderer of the legend, and behind him the mysterious human combination of opposites—opposites in meaning and in fact. And so the character may fluctuate or the names may vary. It is the theme, the generic side of tragedy, which is important; it is there that the emphasis of the play rests.

FURTHER INTRODUCTORY NOTE, 1991

My version of *Oedipus the King* was written fifty years ago. Of the two other translations which also formerly appeared in this volume, Robert Fitzgerald's *Oedipus at Colonus* is of almost the same vintage and Elizabeth Wyckoff's *Antigone* is more than thirty years old. As the remaining editor of *The Complete Greek*

Tragedies I have been looking through the series, at the suggestion of the Press, and have been making some alterations. Perhaps some of my criticisms may have been misplaced, but certain features of these translations by Wyckoff and Fitzgerald seemed unsatisfactory. Besides, despite the small inconsistencies in the story of the three plays, which I mentioned earlier, there is certainly a unity of tone and style in these Theban plays that greatly favors the same translator for all of them. So I have translated the *Antigone* and the *Oedipus at Colonus* and have substituted them for the previous renderings of Wyckoff and Fitzgerald.

Though the numbered lines of my *Oedipus the King* appear to match fairly thoroughly those of the Greek text, I have not been so successful with the combination of the Greek and the English in these last two plays. Often I have needed more space than the limitation of a line would allow. More commonly I have written two or more short lines for one of the Greek in the interest of vividness or other dramatic reasons. This has caused a confusion that I had not anticipated, and a lot of complaints. So from this reprint on, the numbering in the margins of these versions of the *Antigone* and *Oedipus at Colonnus* has been changed to correspond to that of the Greek text. With the anchor of the Greek lines, it is comparatively simple for the reader to notice where he or she is in the text, and notice (I hope without resentment) the purely formal difference of the number of lines rendering it.

Some years ago the Court Theatre asked Wendy Doniger and me to do a new prose version of the *Antigone* for their repertory company. We worked in very close collaboration with the actors. Because the Court Theatre rendering was in prose, and all the other plays in the series of *The Complete Greek Tragedies* were overwhelmingly in verse, I decided to write the *Antigone* and *Oedipus at Colonnus* in my new translation in verse. But I owe a great deal to the earlier prose version of the *Antigone*, which I gladly acknowledge, and to Wendy Doniger's participation in it.

UNIVERSITY OF CHICAGO   DAVID GRENE

OEDIPUS THE KING

CHARACTERS

Oedipus, King of Thebes

Jocasta, His Wife

Creon, His Brother-in-Law

Teiresias, an Old Blind Prophet

A Priest

First Messenger

Second Messenger

A Herdsman

A Chorus of Old Men of Thebes

OEDIPUS THE KING

SCENE: *In front of the palace of Oedipus at Thebes. To the right of the stage near the altar stands the Priest with a crowd of children. Oedipus emerges from the central door.*

Oedipus

Children, young sons and daughters of old Cadmus,
why do you sit here with your suppliant crowns?
The town is heavy with a mingled burden
of sounds and smells, of groans and hymns and incense;   5
I did not think it fit that I should hear
of this from messengers but came myself,—
I Oedipus whom all men call the Great.

                             (He turns to the Priest.)

You're old and they are young; come, speak for them.
What do you fear or want, that you sit here   10
suppliant? Indeed I'm willing to give all
that you may need; I would be very hard
should I not pity suppliants like these.

Priest

O ruler of my country, Oedipus,
you see our company around the altar;   15
you see our ages; some of us, like these,
who cannot yet fly far, and some of us
heavy with age; these children are the chosen
among the young, and I the priest of Zeus.
Within the market place sit others crowned   20
with suppliant garlands, at the double shrine
of Pallas and the temple where Ismenus
gives oracles by fire. King, you yourself
have seen our city reeling like a wreck
already; it can scarcely lift its prow
out of the depths, out of the bloody surf.

A blight is on the fruitful plants of the earth,   25
A blight is on the cattle in the fields,
a blight is on our women that no children
are born to them; a God that carries fire,
a deadly pestilence, is on our town,
strikes us and spares not, and the house of Cadmus
is emptied of its people while black Death
grows rich in groaning and in lamentation.   30
We have not come as suppliants to this altar
because we thought of you as of a God,
but rather judging you the first of men
in all the chances of this life and when
we mortals have to do with more than man.
You came and by your coming saved our city,   35
freed us from tribute which we paid of old
to the Sphinx, cruel singer. This you did
in virtue of no knowledge we could give you,
in virtue of no teaching; it was God
that aided you, men say, and you are held
with God's assistance to have saved our lives.
Now Oedipus, Greatest in all men's eyes,   40
here falling at your feet we all entreat you,
find us some strength for rescue.
Perhaps you'll hear a wise word from some God,
perhaps you will learn something from a man
(for I have seen that for the skilled of practice
the outcome of their counsels live the most).   45
Noblest of men, go, and raise up our city,
go,—and give heed. For now this land of ours
calls you its savior since you saved it once.
So, let us never speak about your reign
as of a time when first our feet were set
secure on high, but later fell to ruin.   50
Raise up our city, save it and raise it up.
Once you have brought us luck with happy omen;
be no less now in fortune.

If you will rule this land, as now you rule it,
better to rule it full of men than empty.   55
For neither tower nor ship is anything
when empty, and none live in it together.

Oedipus

I pity you, children. You have come full of longing,
but I have known the story before you told it
only too well. I know you are all sick,
yet there is not one of you, sick though you are,   60
that is as sick as I myself.
Your several sorrows each have single scope
and touch but one of you. My spirit groans
for city and myself and you at once.
You have not roused me like a man from sleep;   65
know that I have given many tears to this,
gone many ways wandering in thought,
but as I thought I found only one remedy
and that I took. I sent Menoeceus' son
Creon, Jocasta's brother, to Apollo,   70
to his Pythian temple,
that he might learn there by what act or word
I could save this city. As I count the days,
it vexes me what ails him; he is gone
far longer than he needed for the journey.   75
But when he comes, then, may I prove a villain,
if I shall not do all the God commands.

Priest

Thanks for your gracious words. Your servants here
signal that Creon is this moment coming.

Oedipus

His face is bright. O holy Lord Apollo,   80
grant that his news too may be bright for us
and bring us safety.

Priest

It is happy news,
I think, for else his head would not be crowned
with sprigs of fruitful laurel.

Oedipus

We will know soon,
he's within hail. Lord Creon, my good brother,   85
what is the word you bring us from the God?

(Creon enters.)

Creon

A good word,—for things hard to bear themselves
if in the final issue all is well
I count complete good fortune.

Oedipus

What do you mean?
What you have said so far
leaves me uncertain whether to trust or fear.   90

Creon

If you will hear my news before these others
I am ready to speak, or else to go within.

Oedipus

Speak it to all;
the grief I bear, I bear it more for these
than for my own heart.

Creon

I will tell you, then,   95
what I heard from the God.
King Phoebus in plain words commanded us
to drive out a pollution from our land,
pollution grown ingrained within the land;
drive it out, said the God, not cherish it,
till it's past cure.

Oedipus

What is the rite
of purification? How shall it be done?

Creon

   By banishing a man, or expiation 100
   of blood by blood, since it is murder guilt
   which holds our city in this destroying storm.

Oedipus

   Who is this man whose fate the God pronounces?

Creon

   My Lord, before you piloted the state
   we had a king called Laius.

Oedipus

   I know of him by hearsay. I have not seen him. 105

Creon

   The God commanded clearly: let some one
   punish with force this dead man's murderers.

Oedipus

   Where are they in the world? Where would a trace
   of this old crime be found? It would be hard
   to guess where.

Creon

              The clue is in this land; 110
   that which is sought is found;
   the unheeded thing escapes:
   so said the God.

Oedipus

             Was it at home,
   or in the country that death came upon him,
   or in another country travelling?

Creon

   He went, he said himself, upon an embassy,
   but never returned when he set out from home. 115

Oedipus

   Was there no messenger, no fellow traveller
   who knew what happened? Such a one might tell
   something of use.

Creon

They were all killed save one. He fled in terror
and he could tell us nothing in clear terms
of what he knew, nothing, but one thing only.

Oedipus

What was it?   120
If we could even find a slim beginning
in which to hope, we might discover much.

Creon

This man said that the robbers they encountered
were many and the hands that did the murder
were many; it was no man's single power.

Oedipus

How could a robber dare a deed like this
were he not helped with money from the city,
money and treachery?   125

Creon

                              That indeed was thought.
But Laius was dead and in our trouble
there was none to help.

Oedipus

What trouble was so great to hinder you
inquiring out the murder of your king?

Creon

The riddling Sphinx induced us to neglect   130
mysterious crimes and rather seek solution
of troubles at our feet.

Oedipus

I will bring this to light again. King Phoebus
fittingly took this care about the dead,
and you too fittingly.
And justly you will see in me an ally,   135
a champion of my country and the God.
For when I drive pollution from the land

I will not serve a distant friend's advantage,
but act in my own interest. Whoever
he was that killed the king may readily
wish to dispatch me with his murderous hand;   140
so helping the dead king I help myself.

Come, children, take your suppliant boughs and go;
up from the altars now. Call the assembly
and let it meet upon the understanding
that I'll do everything. God will decide   145
whether we prosper or remain in sorrow.

Priest

   Rise, children—it was this we came to seek,
which of himself the king now offers us.
May Phoebus who gave us the oracle
come to our rescue and stay the plague.   150

                         (Exeunt all but the Chorus.)

Chorus

   Strophe

What is the sweet spoken word of God from the shrine of Pytho
   rich in gold
that has come to glorious Thebes?
I am stretched on the rack of doubt, and terror and trembling
   hold
my heart, O Delian Healer, and I worship full of fears
for what doom you will bring to pass, new or renewed in the   155
   revolving years.
Speak to me, immortal voice,
child of golden Hope.

   Antistrophe

First I call on you, Athene, deathless daughter of Zeus,
and Artemis, Earth Upholder,   160
who sits in the midst of the market place in the throne which
   men call Fame,
and Phoebus, the Far Shooter, three averters of Fate,

come to us now, if ever before, when ruin rushed upon the state, 165
you drove destruction's flame away
out of our land.

Strophe
Our sorrows defy number;
all the ship's timbers are rotten;
taking of thought is no spear for the driving away of the plague. 170
There are no growing children in this famous land;
there are no women bearing the pangs of childbirth.
You may see them one with another, like birds swift on the
    wing, 175
quicker than fire unmastered,
speeding away to the coast of the Western God.

Antistrophe
In the unnumbered deaths
of its people the city dies;
those children that are born lie dead on the naked earth
unpitied, spreading contagion of death; and grey haired mothers
    and wives
everywhere stand at the altar's edge, suppliant, moaning; 182–85
the hymn to the healing God rings out but with it the wailing
    voices are blended.
From these our sufferings grant us, O golden Daughter of Zeus,
glad-faced deliverance.

Strophe
There is no clash of brazen shields but our fight is with the War
    God,
a War God ringed with the cries of men, a savage God who burns 191
    us;
grant that he turn in racing course backwards out of our coun-
    try's bounds
to the great palace of Amphitrite or where the waves of the 195
    Thracian sea
deny the stranger safe anchorage.
Whatsoever escapes the night

at last the light of day revisits;
so smite the War God, Father Zeus,
beneath your thunderbolt,
for you are the Lord of the lightning, the lightning that
    carries fire.   200

Antistrophe
And your unconquered arrow shafts, winged by the golden
    corded bow,
Lycean King, I beg to be at our side for help;   205
and the gleaming torches of Artemis with which she scours the
    Lycean hills,
and I call on the God with the turban of gold, who gave his name
    to this country of ours,   210
the Bacchic God with the wind flushed face,
Evian One, who travel
with the Maenad company,
combat the God that burns us
with your torch of pine;
for the God that is our enemy is a God unhonoured among the   215
    Gods.

                               (*Oedipus returns.*)

Oedipus
For what you ask me—if you will hear my words,
and hearing welcome them and fight the plague,
you will find strength and lightening of your load.

Hark to me; what I say to you, I say
as one that is a stranger to the story
as stranger to the deed. For I would not   220
be far upon the track if I alone
were tracing it without a clue. But now,
since after all was finished, I became
a citizen among you, citizens—
now I proclaim to all the men of Thebes:
who so among you knows the murderer   225
by whose hand Laius, son of Labdacus,

died—I command him to tell everything
to me,—yes, though he fears himself to take the blame
on his own head; for bitter punishment
he shall have none, but leave this land unharmed.
Or if he knows the murderer, another,   230
a foreigner, still let him speak the truth.
For I will pay him and be grateful, too.
But if you shall keep silence, if perhaps
some one of you, to shield a guilty friend,
or for his own sake shall reject my words—
hear what I shall do then: 235
I forbid that man, whoever he be, my land,
my land where I hold sovereignty and throne;
and I forbid any to welcome him
or cry him greeting or make him a sharer   240
in sacrifice or offering to the Gods,
or give him water for his hands to wash.
I command all to drive him from their homes,
since he is our pollution, as the oracle
of Pytho's God proclaimed him now to me.
So I stand forth a champion of the God
and of the man who died.   245
Upon the murderer I invoke this curse—
whether he is one man and all unknown,
or one of many—may he wear out his life
· in misery to miserable doom!
If with my knowledge he lives at my hearth   250
I pray that I myself may feel my curse.
On you I lay my charge to fulfill all this
for me, for the God, and for this land of ours
destroyed and blighted, by the God forsaken.

Even were this no matter of God's ordinance   255
it would not fit you so to leave it lie,
unpurified, since a good man is dead
and one that was a king. Search it out.

Since I am now the holder of his office,
and have his bed and wife that once was his,   260
and had his line not been unfortunate
we would have common children—(fortune leaped
upon his head)—because of all these things,
I fight in his defence as for my father,
and I shall try all means to take the murderer   265
of Laius the son of Labdacus
the son of Polydorus and before him
of Cadmus and before him of Agenor.
Those who do not obey me, may the Gods
grant no crops springing from the ground they plough   270
nor children to their women! May a fate
like this, or one still worse than this consume them!
For you whom these words please, the other Thebans,
may Justice as your ally and all the Gods
live with you, blessing you now and for ever!   275

Chorus
    As you have held me to my oath, I speak:
    I neither killed the king nor can declare
    the killer; but since Phoebus set the quest
    it is his part to tell who the man is.

Oedipus
    Right; but to put compulsion on the Gods   280
    against their will—no man can do that.

Chorus
    May I then say what I think second best?

Oedipus
    If there's a third best, too, spare not to tell it.

Chorus
    I know that what the Lord Teiresias
    sees, is most often what the Lord Apollo   285
    sees. If you should inquire of this from him
    you might find out most clearly.

Oedipus
Even in this my actions have not been sluggard.
On Creon's word I have sent two messengers
and why the prophet is not here already
I have been wondering.

Chorus
His skill apart   290
there is besides only an old faint story.

Oedipus
What is it?
I look at every story.

Chorus
It was said
that he was killed by certain wayfarers.

Oedipus
I heard that, too, but no one saw the killer.

Chorus
Yet if he has a share of fear at all,
his courage will not stand firm, hearing your curse.   295

Oedipus
The man who in the doing did not shrink
will fear no word.

Chorus
Here comes his prosecutor:
led by your men the godly prophet comes
in whom alone of mankind truth is native.

(Enter Teiresias, led by a little boy.)

Oedipus
Teiresias, you are versed in everything,   300
things teachable and things not to be spoken,
things of the heaven and earth-creeping things.
You have no eyes but in your mind you know
with what a plague our city is afflicted.
My lord, in you alone we find a champion,

in you alone one that can rescue us.
Perhaps you have not heard the messengers,   305
but Phoebus sent in answer to our sending
an oracle declaring that our freedom
from this disease would only come when we
should learn the names of those who killed King Laius,
and kill them or expel from our country.
Do not begrudge us oracles from birds,   310
or any other way of prophecy
within your skill; save yourself and the city,
save me; redeem the debt of our pollution
that lies on us because of this dead man.
We are in your hands; pains are most nobly taken
to help another when you have means and power.   315

Teiresias
    Alas, how terrible is wisdom when
    it brings no profit to the man that's wise!
    This I knew well, but had forgotten it,
    else I would not have come here.

Oedipus
                        What is this?
    How sad you are now you have come!

Teiresias
                        Let me
    go home. It will be easiest for us both   320
    to bear our several destinies to the end
    if you will follow my advice.

Oedipus
                        You'd rob us
    of this your gift of prophecy? You talk
    as one who had no care for law nor love
    for Thebes who reared you.

Teiresias
    Yes, but I see that even your own words
    miss the mark; therefore I must fear for mine.   325

Oedipus

    For God's sake if you know of anything,
    do not turn from us; all of us kneel to you,
    all of us here, your suppliants.

Teiresias

    All of you here know nothing. I will not
    bring to the light of day my troubles, mine—
    rather than call them yours.

Oedipus

                  What do you mean?
    You know of something but refuse to speak.   330
    Would you betray us and destroy the city?

Teiresias

    I will not bring this pain upon us both,
    neither on you nor on myself. Why is it
    you question me and waste your labour? I
    will tell you nothing.

Oedipus

    You would provoke a stone! Tell us, you villain,   335
    tell us, and do not stand there quietly
    unmoved and balking at the issue.

Teiresias

    You blame my temper but you do not see
    your own that lives within you; it is me
    you chide.

Oedipus

    Who would not feel his temper rise
    at words like these with which you shame our city?   340

Teiresias

    Of themselves things will come, although I hide them
    and breathe no word of them.

Oedipus

                Since they will come
    tell them to me.

Teiresias

I will say nothing further.
Against this answer let your temper rage
as wildly as you will.

Oedipus

Indeed I am   345
so angry I shall not hold back a jot
of what I think. For I would have you know
I think you were complotter of the deed
and doer of the deed save in so far
as for the actual killing. Had you had eyes
I would have said alone you murdered him.

Teiresias

Yes? Then I warn you faithfully to keep   350
the letter of your proclamation and
from this day forth to speak no word of greeting
to these nor me; you are the land's pollution.

Oedipus

How shamelessly you started up this taunt!
How do you think you will escape?   355

Teiresias

I have.
I have escaped; the truth is what I cherish
and that's my strength.

Oedipus

And who has taught you truth?
Not your profession surely!

Teiresias

You have taught me,
for you have made me speak against my will.

Oedipus

Speak what? Tell me again that I may learn it better.

Teiresias

Did you not understand before or would you
provoke me into speaking?   360

Oedipus

                I did not grasp it,
not so to call it known. Say it again.

Teiresias

    I say you are the murderer of the king
whose murderer you seek.

Oedipus

                    Not twice you shall
say calumnies like this and stay unpunished.

Teiresias

    Shall I say more to tempt your anger more?

Oedipus

    As much as you desire; it will be said   365
in vain.

Teiresias

            I say that with those you love best
you live in foulest shame unconsciously
and do not see where you are in calamity.

Oedipus

    Do you imagine you can always talk
like this, and live to laugh at it hereafter?

Teiresias

    Yes, if the truth has anything of strength.

Oedipus

    It has, but not for you; it has no strength   370
for you because you are blind in mind and ears
as well as in your eyes.

Teiresias

              You are a poor wretch
to taunt me with the very insults which
every one soon will heap upon yourself.

Oedipus

    Your life is one long night so that you cannot
hurt me or any other who sees the light.   375

Teiresias

It is not fate that I should be your ruin,
Apollo is enough; it is his care
to work this out.

Oedipus

Was this your own design
or Creon's?

Teiresias

Creon is no hurt to you,
but you are to yourself.

Oedipus

Wealth, sovereignty and skill outmatching skill   380
for the contrivance of an envied life!
Great store of jealousy fill your treasury chests,
if my friend Creon, friend from the first and loyal,   385
thus secretly attacks me, secretly
desires to drive me out and secretly
suborns this juggling, trick devising quack,
this wily beggar who has only eyes
for his own gains, but blindness in his skill.
For, tell me, where have you seen clear, Teiresias,   390
with your prophetic eyes? When the dark singer,
the sphinx, was in your country, did you speak
word of deliverance to its citizens?
And yet the riddle's answer was not the province
of a chance comer. It was a prophet's task
and plainly you had no such gift of prophecy   395
from birds nor otherwise from any God
to glean a word of knowledge. But I came,
Oedipus, who knew nothing, and I stopped her.
I solved the riddle by my wit alone.
Mine was no knowledge got from birds. And now
you would expel me,
because you think that you will find a place   400
by Creon's throne. I think you will be sorry,

both you and your accomplice, for your plot
to drive me out. And did I not regard you
as an old man, some suffering would have taught you
that what was in your heart was treason.

Chorus

We look at this man's words and yours, my king,
and we find both have spoken them in anger.   405
We need no angry words but only thought
how we may best hit the God's meaning for us.

Teiresias

If you are king, at least I have the right
no less to speak in my defence against you.
Of that much I am master. I am no slave   410
of yours, but Loxias', and so I shall not
enroll myself with Creon for my patron.
Since you have taunted me with being blind,
here is my word for you.
You have your eyes but see not where you are
in sin, nor where you live, nor whom you live with.
Do you know who your parents are? Unknowing   415
you are an enemy to kith and kin
in death, beneath the earth, and in this life.
A deadly footed, double striking curse,
from father and mother both, shall drive you forth
out of this land, with darkness on your eyes,
that now have such straight vision. Shall there be
a place will not be harbour to your cries,   420
a corner of Cithaeron will not ring
in echo to your cries, soon, soon,—
when you shall learn the secret of your marriage,
which steered you to a haven in this house,—
haven no haven, after lucky voyage?
And of the multitude of other evils
establishing a grim equality
between you and your children, you know nothing.   425

So, muddy with contempt my words and Creon's!
Misery shall grind no man as it will you.

Oedipus

Is it endurable that I should hear
such words from him? Go and a curse go with you!   430
Quick, home with you! Out of my house at once!

Teiresias

I would not have come either had you not called me.

Oedipus

I did not know then you would talk like a fool—
or it would have been long before I called you.

Teiresias

I am a fool then, as it seems to you—   435
but to the parents who have bred you, wise.

Oedipus

What parents? Stop! Who are they of all the world?

Teiresias

This day will show your birth and will destroy you.

Oedipus

How needlessly your riddles darken everything.

Teiresias

But it's in riddle answering you are strongest.   440

Oedipus

Yes. Taunt me where you will find me great.

Teiresias

It is this very luck that has destroyed you.

Oedipus

I do not care, if it has saved this city.

Teiresias

Well, I will go. Come, boy, lead me away.

Oedipus

Yes, lead him off. So long as you are here,   445

you'll be a stumbling block and a vexation;
once gone, you will not trouble me again.

Teiresias
                              I have said
what I came here to say not fearing your
countenance: there is no way you can hurt me.
I tell you, king, this man, this murderer
(whom you have long declared you are in search of,
indicting him in threatening proclamation   450
as murderer of Laius)—he is here.
In name he is a stranger among citizens
but soon he will be shown to be a citizen
true native Theban, and he'll have no joy
of the discovery: blindness for sight
and beggary for riches his exchange,   455
he shall go journeying to a foreign country
tapping his way before him with a stick.
He shall be proved father and brother both
to his own children in his house; to her
that gave him birth, a son and husband both;
a fellow sower in his father's bed
with that same father that he murdered.
Go within, reckon that out, and if you find me   460
mistaken, say I have no skill in prophecy.

                    (*Exeunt separately Teiresias and Oedipus.*)
Chorus
    Strophe
Who is the man proclaimed
by Delphi's prophetic rock
as the bloody handed murderer,   465
the doer of deeds that none dare name?
Now is the time for him to run
with a stronger foot
than Pegasus
for the child of Zeus leaps in arms upon him   470
with fire and the lightning bolt,

and terribly close on his heels
are the Fates that never miss.

Antistrophe
Lately from snowy Parnassus
clearly the voice flashed forth,
bidding each Theban track him down,   475
the unknown murderer.
In the savage forests he lurks and in
the caverns like
the mountain bull.
He is sad and lonely, and lonely his feet
that carry him far from the navel of earth;   480
but its prophecies, ever living,
flutter around his head.

Strophe
The augur has spread confusion,
terrible confusion;
I do not approve what was said   485
nor can I deny it.
I do not know what to say;
I am in a flutter of foreboding;
I never heard in the present
nor past of a quarrel between   490
the sons of Labdacus and Polybus,
that I might bring as proof
in attacking the popular fame
of Oedipus, seeking
to take vengeance for undiscovered
death in the line of Labdacus.   495

Antistrophe
Truly Zeus and Apollo are wise
and in human things all knowing;
but amongst men there is no   500
distinct judgment, between the prophet
and me—which of us is right.

One man may pass another in wisdom
but I would never agree
with those that find fault with the king
till I should see the word
proved right beyond doubt. For once
in visible form the Sphinx
came on him and all of us
saw his wisdom and in that test
he saved the city. So he will not be condemned by my mind.   512

                                        (*Enter Creon.*)

Creon

   Citizens, I have come because I heard
deadly words spread about me, that the king
accuses me. I cannot take that from him.
If he believes that in these present troubles   515
he has been wronged by me in word or deed
I do not want to live on with the burden
of such a scandal on me. The report   520
injures me doubly and most vitally—
for I'll be called a traitor to my city
and traitor also to my friends and you.

Chorus

   Perhaps it was a sudden gust of anger
that forced that insult from him, and no judgment.

Creon

   But did he say that it was in compliance   525
with schemes of mine that the seer told him lies?

Chorus

   Yes, he said that, but why, I do not know.

Creon

   Were his eyes straight in his head? Was his mind right
when he accused me in this fashion?

Chorus

   I do not know; I have no eyes to see   530
what princes do. Here comes the king himself.

(Enter Oedipus.)

Oedipus

You, sir, how is it you come here? Have you so much
brazen-faced daring that you venture in
my house although you are proved manifestly
the murderer of that man, and though you tried,
openly, highway robbery of my crown?   535
For God's sake, tell me what you saw in me,
what cowardice or what stupidity,
that made you lay a plot like this against me?
Did you imagine I should not observe
the crafty scheme that stole upon me or
seeing it, take no means to counter it?   540
Was it not stupid of you to make the attempt,
to try to hunt down royal power without
the people at your back or friends? For only
with the people at your back or money can
the hunt end in the capture of a crown.

Creon

Do you know what you're doing? Will you listen
to words to answer yours, and then pass judgment?

Oedipus

You're quick to speak, but I am slow to grasp you,   545
for I have found you dangerous,—and my foe.

Creon

First of all hear what I shall say to that.

Oedipus

At least don't tell me that you are not guilty.

Creon

If you think obstinacy without wisdom
a valuable possession, you are wrong.   550

Oedipus

And you are wrong if you believe that one,
a criminal, will not be punished only
because he is my kinsman.

Creon

                  This is but just—
but tell me, then, of what offense I'm guilty?

Oedipus

Did you or did you not urge me to send   555
to this prophetic mumbler?

Creon

                     I did indeed,
and I shall stand by what I told you.

Oedipus

How long ago is it since Laius. . . .

Creon

What about Laius? I don't understand.

Oedipus

Vanished—died—was murdered?   560

Creon

                 It is long,
a long, long time to reckon.

Oedipus

               Was this prophet
in the profession then?

Creon

              He was, and honoured
as highly as he is today.

Oedipus

At that time did he say a word about me?

Creon

Never, at least when I was near him.   565

Oedipus

You never made a search for the dead man?

Creon

We searched, indeed, but never learned of anything.

Oedipus

Why did our wise old friend not say this then?

Creon
I don't know; and when I know nothing, I
usually hold my tongue.

Oedipus
You know this much, 570
and can declare this much if you are loyal.

Creon
What is it? If I know, I'll not deny it.

Oedipus
That he would not have said that I killed Laius
had he not met you first.

Creon
You know yourself
whether he said this, but I demand that I 575
should hear as much from you as you from me.

Oedipus
Then hear,—I'll not be proved a murderer.

Creon
Well, then. You're married to my sister.

Oedipus
Yes,
that I am not disposed to deny.

Creon
You rule
this country giving her an equal share
in the government?

Oedipus
Yes, everything she wants 580
she has from me.

Creon
And I, as thirdsman to you,
am rated as the equal of you two?

Oedipus
Yes, and it's there you've proved yourself false friend.

Creon

Not if you will reflect on it as I do.
Consider, first, if you think any one
would choose to rule and fear rather than rule   585
and sleep untroubled by a fear if power
were equal in both cases. I, at least,
I was not born with such a frantic yearning
to be a king—but to do what kings do.
And so it is with every one who has learned
wisdom and self-control. As it stands now,
the prizes are all mine—and without fear.   590
But if I were the king myself, I must
do much that went against the grain.
How should despotic rule seem sweeter to me
than painless power and an assured authority?
I am not so besotted yet that I
want other honours than those that come with profit.   595
Now every man's my pleasure; every man greets me;
now those who are your suitors fawn on me,—
success for them depends upon my favour.
Why should I let all this go to win that?
My mind would not be traitor if it's wise;   600
I am no treason lover, of my nature,
nor would I ever dare to join a plot.
Prove what I say. Go to the oracle
at Pytho and inquire about the answers,
if they are as I told you. For the rest,   605
if you discover I laid any plot
together with the seer, kill me, I say,
not only by your vote but by my own.
But do not charge me on obscure opinion
without some proof to back it. It's not just
lightly to count your knaves as honest men,   610
nor honest men as knaves. To throw away
an honest friend is, as it were, to throw
your life away, which a man loves the best.

In time you will know all with certainty;
time is the only test of honest men,
one day is space enough to know a rogue.   615

Chorus

His words are wise, king, if one fears to fall.
Those who are quick of temper are not safe.

Oedipus

When he that plots against me secretly
moves quickly, I must quickly counterplot.
If I wait taking no decisive measure   620
his business will be done, and mine be spoiled.

Creon

What do you want to do then? Banish me?

Oedipus

No, certainly; kill you, not banish you.[1]

Creon

I do not think that you've your wits about you.   626

Oedipus

For my own interests, yes.

Creon

                    But for mine, too,
you should think equally.

Oedipus

                    You are a rogue.

Creon

Suppose you do not understand?

Oedipus

                    But yet
I must be ruler.

1. Two lines omitted here owing to the confusion in the dialogue consequent on
the loss of a third line. The lines as they stand in Jebb's edition (1902) are:

Oed.: That you may show what manner of thing is envy.
Creon: You speak as one that will not yield or trust.
[Oed. lost line.]

Creon

> Not if you rule badly.

Oedipus

> O, city, city!

Creon

> I too have some share   630
> in the city; it is not yours alone.

Chorus

> Stop, my lords! Here—and in the nick of time
> I see Jocasta coming from the house;
> with her help lay the quarrel that now stirs you.

> *(Enter Jocasta.)*

Jocasta

> For shame! Why have you raised this foolish squabbling
> brawl? Are you not ashamed to air your private   635
> griefs when the country's sick? Go in, you, Oedipus,
> and you, too, Creon, into the house. Don't magnify
> your nothing troubles.

Creon

> Sister, Oedipus,
> your husband, thinks he has the right to do
> terrible wrongs—he has but to choose between   640
> two terrors: banishing or killing me.

Oedipus

> He's right, Jocasta; for I find him plotting
> with knavish tricks against my person.

Creon

> That God may never bless me! May I die
> accursed, if I have been guilty of   645
> one tittle of the charge you bring against me!

Jocasta

> I beg you, Oedipus, trust him in this,
> spare him for the sake of this his oath to God,
> for my sake, and the sake of those who stand here.

Chorus

Be gracious, be merciful,   649
we beg of you.

Oedipus

In what would you have me yield?

Chorus

He has been no silly child in the past.
He is strong in his oath now.
Spare him.

Oedipus

Do you know what you ask?

Chorus

Yes.

Oedipus

Tell me then.

Chorus

He has been your friend before all men's eyes; do not cast him   656
away dishonoured on an obscure conjecture.

Oedipus

I would have you know that this request of yours
really requests my death or banishment.

Chorus

May the Sun God, king of Gods, forbid! May I die without God's   660
blessing, without friends' help, if I had any such thought. But my
spirit is broken by my unhappiness for my wasting country; and   665
this would but add troubles amongst ourselves to the other
troubles.

Oedipus

Well, let him go then—if I must die ten times for it,   669
or be sent out dishonoured into exile.
It is your lips that prayed for him I pitied,
not his; wherever he is, I shall hate him.

Creon

I see you sulk in yielding and you're dangerous
when you are out of temper; natures like yours
are justly heaviest for themselves to bear.   675

Oedipus

Leave me alone! Take yourself off, I tell you.

Creon

I'll go, you have not known me, but they have,
and they have known my innocence.

                                                                (*Exit.*)

Chorus

Won't you take him inside, lady?

Jocasta

Yes, when I've found out what was the matter.   680

Chorus

There was some misconceived suspicion of a story, and on the
other side the sting of injustice.

Jocasta

So, on both sides?

Chorus

Yes.

Jocasta

What was the story?

Chorus

I think it best, in the interests of the country, to leave it where   685
it ended.

Oedipus

You see where you have ended, straight of judgment
although you are, by softening my anger.

Chorus

Sir, I have said before and I say again—be sure that I would have   689
been proved a madman, bankrupt in sane council, if I should put
you away, you who steered the country I love safely when she

was crazed with troubles. God grant that now, too, you may   695
prove a fortunate guide for us.

Jocasta
Tell me, my lord, I beg of you, what was it
that roused your anger so?

Oedipus
       Yes, I will tell you.   700
I honour you more than I honour them.
It was Creon and the plots he laid against me.

Jocasta
Tell me—if you can clearly tell the quarrel—

Oedipus
      Creon says
that I'm the murderer of Laius.

Jocasta
Of his own knowledge or on information?

Oedipus
He sent this rascal prophet to me, since   705
he keeps his own mouth clean of any guilt.

Jocasta
Do not concern yourself about this matter;
listen to me and learn that human beings
have no part in the craft of prophecy.
Of that I'll show you a short proof.   710
There was an oracle once that came to Laius,—
I will not say that it was Phoebus' own,
but it was from his servants—and it told him
that it was fate that he should die a victim
at the hands of his own son, a son to be born
of Laius and me. But, see now, he,
the king, was killed by foreign highway robbers   715
at a place where three roads meet—so goes the story;
and for the son—before three days were out
after his birth King Laius pierced his ankles

and by the hands of others cast him forth
upon a pathless hillside. So Apollo   720
failed to fulfill his oracle to the son,
that he should kill his father, and to Laius
also proved false in that the thing he feared,
death at his son's hands, never came to pass.
So clear in this case were the oracles,
so clear and false. Give them no heed, I say;
what God discovers need of, easily
he shows to us himself.   725

Oedipus

                    O dear Jocasta,
as I hear this from you, there comes upon me
a wandering of the soul—I could run mad.

Jocasta

What trouble is it, that you turn again
and speak like this?

Oedipus

                    I thought I heard you say
that Laius was killed at a crossroads.   730

Jocasta

Yes, that was how the story went and still
that word goes round.

Oedipus

                    Where is this place, Jocasta,
where he was murdered?

Jocasta

                    Phocis is the country
and the road splits there, one of two roads from Delphi,
another comes from Daulia.

Oedipus

                    How long ago is this?   735

Jocasta

The news came to the city just before

you became king and all men's eyes looked to you.
What is it, Oedipus, that's in your mind?

Oedipus

What have you designed, O Zeus, to do with me?

Jocasta

What is the thought that troubles your heart?

Oedipus

Don't ask me yet—tell me of Laius—   740
How did he look? How old or young was he?

Jocasta

He was a tall man and his hair was grizzled
already—nearly white—and in his form
not unlike you.

Oedipus

     O God, I think I have
called curses on myself in ignorance.   745

Jocasta

What do you mean? I am terrified
when I look at you.

Oedipus

     I have a deadly fear
that the old seer had eyes. You'll show me more
if you can tell me one more thing.

Jocasta

      I will.
I'm frightened,—but if I can understand,
I'll tell you all you ask.

Oedipus

     How was his company?   750
Had he few with him when he went this journey,
or many servants, as would suit a prince?

Jocasta

In all there were but five, and among them
a herald; and one carriage for the king.

Oedipus

It's plain—its plain—who was it told you this?   755

Jocasta

The only servant that escaped safe home.

Oedipus

Is he at home now?

Jocasta

      No, when he came home again
and saw you king and Laius was dead,
he came to me and touched my hand and begged   760
that I should send him to the fields to be
my shepherd and so he might see the city
as far off as he might. So I
sent him away. He was an honest man,
as slaves go, and was worthy of far more
than what he asked of me.

Oedipus

O, how I wish that he could come back quickly!   765

Jocasta

He can. Why is your heart so set on this?

Oedipus

O dear Jocasta, I am full of fears
that I have spoken far too much; and therefore
I wish to see this shepherd.

Jocasta

      He will come;
but, Oedipus, I think I'm worthy too
to know what it is that disquiets you.   770

Oedipus

It shall not be kept from you, since my mind
has gone so far with its forebodings. Whom
should I confide in rather than you, who is there
of more importance to me who have passed
through such a fortune?

Polybus was my father, king of Corinth,
and Merope, the Dorian, my mother. 775
I was held greatest of the citizens
in Corinth till a curious chance befell me
as I shall tell you—curious, indeed,
but hardly worth the store I set upon it.
There was a dinner and at it a man,
a drunken man, accused me in his drink 780
of being bastard. I was furious
but held my temper under for that day.
Next day I went and taxed my parents with it;
they took the insult very ill from him,
the drunken fellow who had uttered it.
So I was comforted for their part, but 785
still this thing rankled always, for the story
crept about widely. And I went at last
to Pytho, though my parents did not know.
But Phoebus sent me home again unhonoured
in what I came to learn, but he foretold 790
other and desperate horrors to befall me,
that I was fated to lie with my mother,
and show to daylight an accursed breed
which men would not endure, and I was doomed
to be murderer of the father that begot me.
When I heard this I fled, and in the days
that followed I would measure from the stars 795
the whereabouts of Corinth—yes, I fled
to somewhere where I should not see fulfilled
the infamies told in that dreadful oracle.
And as I journeyed I came to the place
where, as you say, this king met with his death.
Jocasta, I will tell you the whole truth. 800
When I was near the branching of the crossroads,
going on foot, I was encountered by
a herald and a carriage with a man in it,
just as you tell me. He that led the way

and the old man himself wanted to thrust me 805
out of the road by force. I became angry
and struck the coachman who was pushing me.
When the old man saw this he watched his moment,
and as I passed he struck me from his carriage,
full on the head with his two pointed goad.
But he was paid in full and presently 810
my stick had struck him backwards from the car
and he rolled out of it. And then I killed them
all. If it happened there was any tie
of kinship twixt this man and Laius,
who is then now more miserable than I, 815
what man on earth so hated by the Gods,
since neither citizen nor foreigner
may welcome me at home or even greet me,
but drive me out of doors? And it is I,
I and no other have so cursed myself. 820
And I pollute the bed of him I killed
by the hands that killed him. Was I not born evil?
Am I not utterly unclean? I had to fly
and in my banishment not even see
my kindred nor set foot in my own country,
or otherwise my fate was to be yoked 825
in marriage with my mother and kill my father,
Polybus who begot me and had reared me.
Would not one rightly judge and say that on me
these things were sent by some malignant God?
O no, no, no—O holy majesty 830
of God on high, may I not see that day!
May I be gone out of men's sight before
I see the deadly taint of this disaster
come upon me.

Chorus

    Sir, we too fear these things. But until you see this man face to
face and hear his story, hope. 835

Oedipus

Yes, I have just this much of hope—to wait until the herdsman comes.

Jocasta

And when he comes, what do you want with him?

Oedipus

I'll tell you; if I find that his story is the same as yours, I at least will be clear of this guilt.   840

Jocasta

Why what so particularly did you learn from my story?

Oedipus

You said that he spoke of highway *robbers* who killed Laius. Now if he uses the same number, it was not I who killed him. One man cannot be the same as many. But if he speaks of a man travelling   845
alone, then clearly the burden of the guilt inclines towards me.

Jocasta

Be sure, at least, that this was how he told the story. He cannot unsay it now, for every one in the city heard it—not I alone. But,   850
Oedipus, even if he diverges from what he said then, he shall never prove that the murder of Laius squares rightly with the prophecy—for Loxias declared that the king should be killed by his own son. And that poor creature did not kill him surely,—   855
for he died himself first. So as far as prophecy goes, henceforward I shall not look to the right hand or the left.

Oedipus

Right. But yet, send some one for the peasant to bring him here;   860
do not neglect it.

Jocasta

I will send quickly. Now let me go indoors. I will do nothing except what pleases you.

(Exeunt.)

Chorus

   Strophe
May destiny ever find me

pious in word and deed   865
prescribed by the laws that live on high:
laws begotten in the clear air of heaven,
whose only father is Olympus;
no mortal nature brought them to birth,
no forgetfulness shall lull them to sleep;   870
for God is great in them and grows not old.

Antistrophe
Insolence breeds the tyrant, insolence
if it is glutted with a surfeit, unseasonable, unprofitable,   875
climbs to the roof-top and plunges
sheer down to the ruin that must be,
and there its feet are no service.
But I pray that the God may never   880
abolish the eager ambition that profits the state.
For I shall never cease to hold the God as our protector.

Strophe
If a man walks with haughtiness
of hand or word and gives no heed   885
to Justice and the shrines of Gods
despises—may an evil doom
smite him for his ill-starred pride of heart!—
if he reaps gains without justice
and will not hold from impiety   890
and his fingers itch for untouchable things.
When such things are done, what man shall contrive
to shield his soul from the shafts of the God?
When such deeds are held in honour,   895
why should I honour the Gods in the dance?

Antistrophe
No longer to the holy place,
to the navel of earth I'll go
to worship, nor to Abae
nor to Olympia,   900
unless the oracles are proved to fit,
for all men's hands to point at.

O Zeus, if you are rightly called
the sovereign lord, all-mastering,
let this not escape you nor your ever-living power!   905
The oracles concerning Laius
are old and dim and men regard them not.
Apollo is nowhere clear in honour; God's service perishes.   910

(Enter Jocasta, carrying garlands.)

Jocasta

Princes of the land, I have had the thought to go
to the Gods' temples, bringing in my hand
garlands and gifts of incense, as you see.
For Oedipus excites himself too much
at every sort of trouble, not conjecturing,   915
like a man of sense, what will be from what was,
but he is always at the speaker's mercy,
when he speaks terrors. I can do no good
by my advice, and so I came as suppliant
to you, Lycaean Apollo, who are nearest.
These are the symbols of my prayer and this   920
my prayer: grant us escape free of the curse.
Now when we look to him we are all afraid;
he's pilot of our ship and he is frightened.

(Enter Messenger.)

Messenger

Might I learn from you, sirs, where is the house of Oedipus? Or   925
best of all, if you know, where is the king himself?

Chorus

This is his house and he is within doors. This lady is his wife and
mother of his children.

Messenger

God bless you, lady, and God bless your household! God bless   930
Oedipus' noble wife!

Jocasta

God bless you, sir, for your kind greeting! What do you want
of us that you have come here? What have you to tell us?

« 49 »

Messenger

Good news, lady. Good for your house and for your husband.

Jocasta

What is your news? Who sent you to us?   935

Messenger

I come from Corinth and the news I bring will give you pleasure.
Perhaps a little pain too.

Jocasta

What is this news of double meaning?

Messenger

The people of the Isthmus will choose Oedipus to be their king.   940
That is the rumour there.

Jocasta

But isn't their king still old Polybus?

Messenger

No. He is in his grave. Death has got him.

Jocasta

Is that the truth? Is Oedipus' father dead?

Messenger

May I die myself if it be otherwise!

Jocasta (to a servant)

Be quick and run to the King with the news! O oracles of the   945
Gods, where are you now? It was from this man Oedipus fled, lest
he should be his murderer! And now he is dead, in the course of
nature, and not killed by Oedipus.

                                        (Enter Oedipus.)

Oedipus

Dearest Jocasta, why have you sent for me?   950

Jocasta

Listen to this man and when you hear reflect what is the outcome
of the holy oracles of the Gods.

Oedipus

Who is he? What is his message for me?

Jocasta

He is from Corinth and he tells us that your father Polybus is   955
dead and gone.

Oedipus

What's this you say, sir? Tell me yourself.

Messenger

Since this is the first matter you want clearly told: Polybus has
gone down to death. You may be sure of it.

Oedipus

By treachery or sickness?   960

Messenger

A small thing will put old bodies asleep.

Oedipus

So he died of sickness, it seems,—poor old man!

Messenger

Yes, and of age—the long years he had measured.

Oedipus

Ha! Ha! O dear Jocasta, why should one
look to the Pythian hearth? Why should one look   965
to the birds screaming overhead? They prophesied
that I should kill my father! But he's dead,
and hidden deep in earth, and I stand here
who never laid a hand on spear against him,—
unless perhaps he died of longing for me,
and thus I am his murderer. But they,   970
the oracles, as they stand—he's taken them
away with him, they're dead as he himself is,
and worthless.

Jocasta

                        That I told you before now.

Oedipus

You did, but I was misled by my fear.

Jocasta

Then lay no more of them to heart, not one   975

Oedipus
> But surely I must fear my mother's bed?

Jocasta
> Why should man fear since chance is all in all
> for him, and he can clearly foreknow nothing?
> Best to live lightly, as one can, unthinkingly.
> As to your mother's marriage bed,—don't fear it. 980
> Before this, in dreams too, as well as oracles,
> many a man has lain with his own mother.
> But he to whom such things are nothing bears
> his life most easily.

Oedipus
> All that you say would be said perfectly
> if she were dead; but since she lives I must 985
> still fear, although you talk so well, Jocasta.

Jocasta
> Still in your father's death there's light of comfort?

Oedipus
> Great light of comfort; but I fear the living.

Messenger
> Who is the woman that makes you afraid?

Oedipus
> Merope, old man, Polybus' wife. 990

Messenger
> What about her frightens the queen and you?

Oedipus
> A terrible oracle, stranger, from the Gods.

Messenger
> Can it be told? Or does the sacred law
> forbid another to have knowledge of it?

Oedipus
> O no! Once on a time Loxias said
> that I should lie with my own mother and 995

take on my hands the blood of my own father.
And so for these long years I've lived away
from Corinth; it has been to my great happiness;
but yet it's sweet to see the face of parents.

Messenger

This was the fear which drove you out of Corinth?   1000

Oedipus

Old man, I did not wish to kill my father.

Messenger

Why should I not free you from this fear, sir,
since I have come to you in all goodwill?

Oedipus

You would not find me thankless if you did.

Messenger

Why, it was just for this I brought the news,—   1005
to earn your thanks when you had come safe home.

Oedipus

No, I will never come near my parents.

Messenger

                    Son,
it's very plain you don't know what you're doing.

Oedipus

What do you mean, old man? For God's sake, tell me.

Messenger

If your homecoming is checked by fears like these.   1010

Oedipus

Yes, I'm afraid that Phoebus may prove right.

Messenger

The murder and the incest?

Oedipus

                    Yes, old man;
that is my constant terror.

Messenger
                    Do you know
    that all your fears are empty?

Oedipus
                    How is that,   1015
    if they are father and mother and I their son?

Messenger
    Because Polybus was no kin to you in blood.

Oedipus
    What, was not Polybus my father?

Messenger
    No more than I but just so much.

Oedipus
                    How can
    my father be my father as much as one
    that's nothing to me?

Messenger
                    Neither he nor I   1020
    begat you.

Oedipus
                    Why then did he call me son?

Messenger
    A gift he took you from these hands of mine.

Oedipus
    Did he love so much what he took from another's hand?

Messenger
    His childlessness before persuaded him.

Oedipus
    Was I a child you bought or found when I   1025
    was given to him?

Messenger
                    On Cithaeron's slopes
    in the twisting thickets you were found.

Oedipus

And why
were you a traveller in those parts?

Messenger

I was
in charge of mountain flocks.

Oedipus

You were a shepherd?
A hireling vagrant?

Messenger

Yes, but at least at that time   1030
the man that saved your life, son.

Oedipus

What ailed me when you took me in your arms?

Messenger

In that your ankles should be witnesses.

Oedipus

Why do you speak of that old pain?

Messenger

I loosed you;
the tendons of your feet were pierced and fettered,—

Oedipus

My swaddling clothes brought me a rare disgrace.   1035

Messenger

So that from this you're called your present name.

Oedipus

Was this my father's doing or my mother's?
For God's sake, tell me.

Messenger

I don't know, but he
who gave you to me has more knowledge than I.

Oedipus

You yourself did not find me then? You took me
from someone else?

Messenger

                    Yes, from another shepherd.   1040

Oedipus

  Who was he? Do you know him well enough
  to tell?

Messenger

                  He was called Laius' man.

Oedipus

  You mean the king who reigned here in the old days?

Messenger

  Yes, he was that man's shepherd.

Oedipus

                Is he alive   1045
  still, so that I could see him?

Messenger

              You who live here
  would know that best.

Oedipus

           Do any of you here
  know of this shepherd whom he speaks about
  in town or in the fields? Tell me. It's time   1050
  that this was found out once for all.

Chorus

  I think he is none other than the peasant
  whom you have sought to see already; but
  Jocasta here can tell us best of that.

Oedipus

  Jocasta, do you know about this man
  whom we have sent for? Is he the man he mentions?   1055

Jocasta

  Why ask of whom he spoke? Don't give it heed;
  nor try to keep in mind what has been said.
  It will be wasted labour.

Oedipus
>   With such clues
> I could not fail to bring my birth to light.

Jocasta
> I beg you—do not hunt this out—I beg you,   1060
> if you have any care for your own life.
> What I am suffering is enough.

Oedipus
>   Keep up
> your heart, Jocasta. Though I'm proved a slave,
> thrice slave, and though my mother is thrice slave,
> you'll not be shown to be of lowly lineage.

Jocasta
> O be persuaded by me, I entreat you;
> do not do this.

Oedipus
> I will not be persuaded to let be   1065
> the chance of finding out the whole thing clearly.

Jocasta
> It is because I wish you well that I
> give you this counsel—and it's the best counsel.

Oedipus
> Then the best counsel vexes me, and has
> for some while since.

Jocasta
>   O Oedipus, God help you!
> God keep you from the knowledge of who you are!

Oedipus
> Here, some one, go and fetch the shepherd for me;
> and let her find her joy in her rich family!   1070

Jocasta
> O Oedipus, unhappy Oedipus!
> that is all I can call you, and the last thing
> that I shall ever call you.

>   (*Exit.*)

« 57 »

Chorus

Why has the queen gone, Oedipus, in wild
grief rushing from us? I am afraid that trouble   1075
will break out of this silence.

Oedipus

Break out what will! I at least shall be
willing to see my ancestry, though humble.
Perhaps she is ashamed of my low birth,
for she has all a woman's high-flown pride.
But I account myself a child of Fortune,   1080
beneficent Fortune, and I shall not be
dishonoured. She's the mother from whom I spring;
the months, my brothers, marked me, now as small,
and now again as mighty. Such is my breeding,
and I shall never prove so false to it,   1085
as not to find the secret of my birth.

Chorus

Strophe

If I am a prophet and wise of heart
you shall not fail, Cithaeron,   1090
by the limitless sky, you shall not!—
to know at tomorrow's full moon
that Oedipus honours you,
as native to him and mother and nurse at once;
and that you are honoured in dancing by us, as finding favour in
   sight of our king.
Apollo, to whom we cry, find these things pleasing!

Antistrophe

Who was it bore you, child? One of   1098
the long-lived nymphs who lay with Pan—
the father who treads the hills?
Or was she a bride of Loxias, your mother? The grassy slopes
are all of them dear to him. Or perhaps Cyllene's king   1104
or the Bacchants' God that lives on the tops

of the hills received you a gift from some
one of the Helicon Nymphs, with whom he mostly plays?

(Enter an old man, led by Oedipus' servants.)

Oedipus

If some one like myself who never met him   1110
may make a guess,—I think this is the herdsman,
whom we were seeking. His old age is consonant
with the other. And besides, the men who bring him
I recognize as my own servants. You   1115
perhaps may better me in knowledge since
you've seen the man before.

Chorus

                    You can be sure
I recognize him. For if Laius
had ever an honest shepherd, this was he.

Oedipus

You, sir, from Corinth, I must ask you first,
is this the man you spoke of?   1120

Messenger

                    This is he
before your eyes.

Oedipus

                    Old man, look here at me
and tell me what I ask you. Were you ever
a servant of King Laius?

Herdsman

                    I was,—
no slave he bought but reared in his own house.

Oedipus

What did you do as work? How did you live?

Herdsman

Most of my life was spent among the flocks.   1125

Oedipus

In what part of the country did you live?

Herdsman

Cithaeron and the places near to it.

Oedipus

And somewhere there perhaps you knew this man?

Herdsman

What was his occupation? Who?

Oedipus

This man here,   1130
have you had any dealings with him?

Herdsman

No—
not such that I can quickly call to mind.

Messenger

That is no wonder, master. But I'll make him remember what he
does not know. For I know, that he well knows the country of
Cithaeron, how he with two flocks, I with one kept company for   1135
three years—each year half a year—from spring till autumn time
and then when winter came I drove my flocks to our fold home
again and he to Laius' steadings. Well—am I right or not in what   1140
I said we did?

Herdsman

You're right—although it's a long time ago.

Messenger

Do you remember giving me a child
to bring up as my foster child?

Herdsman

What's this?
Why do you ask this question?

Messenger

Look old man,   1145
here he is—here's the man who was that child!

Herdsman

Death take you! Won't you hold your tongue?

Oedipus
                    No, no,
do not find fault with him, old man. Your words
are more at fault than his.

Herdsman
                    O best of masters,
how do I give offense?

Oedipus
                    When you refuse   1150
to speak about the child of whom he asks you.

Herdsman
He speaks out of his ignorance, without meaning.

Oedipus
If you'll not talk to gratify me, you
will talk with pain to urge you.

Herdsman
                    O please, sir,
don't hurt an old man, sir.

Oedipus (*to the servants*)
                    Here, one of you,
twist his hands behind him.

Herdsman
                    Why, God help me, why?   1155
What do you want to know?

Oedipus
                    You gave a child
to him,—the child he asked you of?

Herdsman
                    I did.
I wish I'd died the day I did.

Oedipus
                    You will
unless you tell me truly.

Herdsman

And I'll die
far worse if I should tell you.

Oedipus

This fellow   1160
is bent on more delays, as it would seem.

Herdsman

O no, no! I have told you that I gave it.

Oedipus

Where did you get this child from? Was it your own or did you
get it from another?

Herdsman

Not
my own at all; I had it from some one.

Oedipus

One of these citizens? or from what house?

Herdsman

O master, please—I beg you, master, please   1165
don't ask me more.

Oedipus

You're a dead man if I
ask you again.

Herdsman

It was one of the children
of Laius.

Oedipus

A slave? Or born in wedlock?

Herdsman

O God, I am on the brink of frightful speech.

Oedipus

And I of frightful hearing. But I must hear.   1170

Herdsman

The child was called his child; but she within,
your wife would tell you best how all this was.

Oedipus
  She gave it to you?

Herdsman
                        Yes, she did, my lord.

Oedipus
  To do what with it?

Herdsman
                        Make away with it.

Oedipus
  She was so hard—its mother?   1175

Herdsman
                  Aye, through fear
  of evil oracles.

Oedipus
                        Which?

Herdsman
                  They said that he
  should kill his parents.

Oedipus
                  How was it that you
  gave it away to this old man?

Herdsman
                  O master,
  I pitied it, and thought that I could send it
  off to another country and this man
  was from another country. But he saved it   1180
  for the most terrible troubles. If you are
  the man he says you are, you're bred to misery.

Oedipus
  O, O, O, they will all come,
  all come out clearly! Light of the sun, let me
  look upon you no more after today!
  I who first saw the light bred of a match
  accursed, and accursed in my living
  with them I lived with, cursed in my killing.   1185

                        (*Exeunt all but the Chorus.*)

Chorus

Strophe

O generations of men, how I
count you as equal with those who live
not at all!
What man, what man on earth wins more   1190
of happiness than a seeming
and after that turning away?
Oedipus, you are my pattern of this,
Oedipus, you and your fate!
Luckless Oedipus, whom of all men
I envy not at all.   1196

Antistrophe

In as much as he shot his bolt
beyond the others and won the prize
of happiness complete—
O Zeus—and killed and reduced to nought
the hooked taloned maid of the riddling speech,
standing a tower against death for my land:
hence he was called my king and hence
was honoured the highest of all
honours; and hence he ruled
in the great city of Thebes.

Strophe

But now whose tale is more miserable?   1204
Who is there lives with a savager fate?
Whose troubles so reverse his life as his?

O Oedipus, the famous prince
for whom a great haven
the same both as father and son
sufficed for generation,
how, O how, have the furrows ploughed
by your father endured to bear you, poor wretch,
and hold their peace so long?

Antistrophe

Time who sees all has found you out   1213
against your will; judges your marriage accursed,
begetter and begot at one in it.

O child of Laius,
would I had never seen you.
I weep for you and cry
a dirge of lamentation.

To speak directly, I drew my breath
from you at the first and so now I lull   1222
my mouth to sleep with your name.

                              (*Enter a second messenger.*)

Second Messenger

O Princes always honoured by our country,
what deeds you'll hear of and what horrors see,
what grief you'll feel, if you as true born Thebans   1225
care for the house of Labdacus's sons.
Phasis nor Ister cannot purge this house,
I think, with all their streams, such things
it hides, such evils shortly will bring forth
into the light, whether they will or not;   1230
and troubles hurt the most
when they prove self-inflicted.

Chorus

What we had known before did not fall short
of bitter groaning's worth; what's more to tell?

Second Messenger

Shortest to hear and tell—our glorious queen   1235
Jocasta's dead.

Chorus

                    Unhappy woman! How?

Second Messenger

By her own hand. The worst of what was done
you cannot know. You did not see the sight.
Yet in so far as I remember it

you'll hear the end of our unlucky queen. 1240
When she came raging into the house she went
straight to her marriage bed, tearing her hair
with both her hands, and crying upon Laius 1245
long dead—Do you remember, Laius,
that night long past which bred a child for us
to send you to your death and leave
a mother making children with her son?
And then she groaned and cursed the bed in which
she brought forth husband by her husband, children 1250
by her own child, an infamous double bond.
How after that she died I do not know,—
for Oedipus distracted us from seeing.
He burst upon us shouting and we looked
to him as he paced frantically around,
begging us always: Give me a sword, I say, 1255
to find this wife no wife, this mother's womb,
this field of double sowing whence I sprang
and where I sowed my children! As he raved
some god showed him the way—none of us there.
Bellowing terribly and led by some 1260
invisible guide he rushed on the two doors,—
wrenching the hollow bolts out of their sockets,
he charged inside. There, there, we saw his wife
hanging, the twisted rope around her neck.
When he saw her, he cried out fearfully 1265
and cut the dangling noose. Then, as she lay,
poor woman, on the ground, what happened after,
was terrible to see. He tore the brooches—
the gold chased brooches fastening her robe—
away from her and lifting them up high
dashed them on his own eyeballs, shrieking out 1270
such things as: they will never see the crime
I have committed or had done upon me!
Dark eyes, now in the days to come look on
forbidden faces, do not recognize

those whom you long for—with such imprecations
he struck his eyes again and yet again   1275
with the brooches. And the bleeding eyeballs gushed
and stained his beard—no sluggish oozing drops
but a black rain and bloody hail poured down.

So it has broken—and not on one head   1280
but troubles mixed for husband and for wife.
The fortune of the days gone by was true
good fortune—but today groans and destruction
and death and shame—of all ills can be named   1285
not one is missing.

Chorus

Is he now in any ease from pain?

Second Messenger

He shouts
for some one to unbar the doors and show him
to all the men of Thebes, his father's killer,
his mother's—no I cannot say the word,
it is unholy—for he'll cast himself,
out of the land, he says, and not remain   1290
to bring a curse upon his house, the curse
he called upon it in his proclamation. But
he wants for strength, aye, and some one to guide him;
his sickness is too great to bear. You, too,
will be shown that. The bolts are opening.   1295
Soon you will see a sight to waken pity
even in the horror of it.

(Enter the blinded Oedipus.)

Chorus

This is a terrible sight for men to see!
I never found a worse!
Poor wretch, what madness came upon you!   1300
What evil spirit leaped upon your life
to your ill-luck—a leap beyond man's strength!
Indeed I pity you, but I cannot

look at you, though there's much I want to ask
and much to learn and much to see.   1305
I shudder at the sight of you.

Oedipus
O, O,
where am I going? Where is my voice   1310
borne on the wind to and fro?
Spirit, how far have you sprung?

Chorus
To a terrible place whereof men's ears
may not hear, nor their eyes behold it.

Oedipus
Darkness!
Horror of darkness enfolding, resistless, unspeakable visitant sped
    by an ill wind in haste!   1315
madness and stabbing pain and memory
of evil deeds I have done!

Chorus
In such misfortunes it's no wonder
if double weighs the burden of your grief.   1320

Oedipus
My friend,
you are the only one steadfast, the only one that attends on me;
you still stay nursing the blind man.
Your care is not unnoticed. I can know   1325
your voice, although this darkness is my world.

Chorus
Doer of dreadful deeds, how did you dare
so far to do despite to your own eyes?
what spirit urged you to it?

Oedipus
It was Apollo, friends, Apollo,
that brought this bitter bitterness, my sorrows to completion.   1330
But the hand that struck me

was none but my own.
Why should I see
whose vision showed me nothing sweet to see?   1335

Chorus

These things are as you say.

Oedipus

What can I see to love?
What greeting can touch my ears with joy?
Take me away, and haste—to a place out of the way!   1340
Take me away, my friends, the greatly miserable,
the most accursed, whom God too hates   1345
above all men on earth!

Chorus

Unhappy in your mind and your misfortune,
would I had never known you!

Oedipus

Curse on the man who took
the cruel bonds from off my legs, as I lay in the field.   1350
He stole me from death and saved me,
no kindly service.
Had I died then
I would not be so burdensome to friends.   1355

Chorus

I, too, could have wished it had been so.

Oedipus

Then I would not have come
to kill my father and marry my mother infamously.
Now I am godless and child of impurity,   1360
begetter in the same seed that created my wretched self.
If there is any ill worse than ill,   1365
that is the lot of Oedipus.

Chorus

I cannot say your remedy was good;
you would be better dead than blind and living.

Oedipus

What I have done here was best done—don't tell me   1370
otherwise, do not give me further counsel.
I do not know with what eyes I could look
upon my father when I die and go
under the earth, nor yet my wretched mother—
those two to whom I have done things deserving
worse punishment than hanging. Would the sight   1375
of children, bred as mine are, gladden me?
No, not these eyes, never. And my city,
its towers and sacred places of the Gods,
of these I robbed my miserable self   1380
when I commanded all to drive *him* out,
the criminal since proved by God impure
and of the race of Laius.
To this guilt I bore witness against myself—
with what eyes shall I look upon my people?   1385
No. If there were a means to choke the fountain
of hearing I would not have stayed my hand
from locking up my miserable carcase,
seeing and hearing nothing; it is sweet   1390
to keep our thoughts out of the range of hurt.

Cithaeron, why did you receive me? why
having received me did you not kill me straight?
And so I had not shown to men my birth.

O Polybus and Corinth and the house,
the old house that I used to call my father's—   1395
what fairness you were nurse to, and what foulness
festered beneath! Now I am found to be
a sinner and a son of sinners. Crossroads,
and hidden glade, oak and the narrow way
at the crossroads, that drank my father's blood   1400
offered you by my hands, do you remember
still what I did as you looked on, and what
I did when I came here? O marriage, marriage!

you bred me and again when you had bred
bred children of your child and showed to men   1405
brides, wives and mothers and the foulest deeds
that can be in this world of ours.

Come—it's unfit to say what is unfit
to do.—I beg of you in God's name hide me   1410
somewhere outside your country, yes, or kill me,
or throw me into the sea, to be forever
out of your sight. Approach and deign to touch me
for all my wretchedness, and do not fear.
No man but I can bear my evil doom.   1415

Chorus

Here Creon comes in fit time to perform
or give advice in what you ask of us.
Creon is left sole ruler in your stead.

Oedipus

Creon! Creon! What shall I say to him?
How can I justly hope that he will trust me?   1420
In what is past I have been proved towards him
an utter liar.

                                        (Enter Creon.)

Creon

                        Oedipus, I've come
not so that I might laugh at you nor taunt you
with evil of the past. But if you still
are without shame before the face of men
reverence at least the flame that gives all life,   1425
our Lord the Sun, and do not show unveiled
to him pollution such that neither land
nor holy rain nor light of day can welcome.

                                        (To a servant.)

Be quick and take him in. It is most decent   1430
that only kin should see and hear the troubles
of kin.

Oedipus
>>>>> I beg you, since you've torn me from
my dreadful expectations and have come
in a most noble spirit to a man
that has used you vilely—do a thing for me.
I shall speak for your own good, not for my own.

Creon
What do you need that you would ask of me?   1435

Oedipus
Drive me from here with all the speed you can
to where I may not hear a human voice.

Creon
Be sure, I would have done this had not I
wished first of all to learn from the God the course
of action I should follow.

Oedipus
>>>>>>> But his word   1440
has been quite clear to let the parricide,
the sinner, die.

Creon
>>>>>> Yes, that indeed was said.
But in the present need we had best discover
what we should do.

Oedipus
>>>>> And will you ask about
a man so wretched?

Creon
>>>>> Now even you will trust   1445
the God.

Oedipus
>>>>> So. I command you—and will beseech you—
to her that lies inside that house give burial
as you would have it; she is yours and rightly
you will perform the rites for her. For me—

never let this my father's city have me   1450
living a dweller in it. Leave me live
in the mountains where Cithaeron is, that's called
my mountain, which my mother and my father
while they were living would have made my tomb.
So I may die by their decree who sought
indeed to kill me. Yet I know this much: 1455
no sickness and no other thing will kill me.
I would not have been saved from death if not
for some strange evil fate. Well, let my fate
go where it will.

       Creon, you need not care   1460
about my sons; they're men and so wherever
they are, they will not lack a livelihood.
But my two girls—so sad and pitiful—
whose table never stood apart from mine,
and everything I touched they always shared—   1465
O Creon, have a thought for them! And most
I wish that you might suffer me to touch them
and sorrow with them.

   (*Enter Antigone and Ismene, Oedipus' two daughters.*)
O my lord! O true noble Creon! Can I   1470
really be touching them, as when I saw?
What shall I say?
Yes, I can hear them sobbing—my two darlings!
and Creon has had pity and has sent me
what I loved most?
Am I right?   1475

Creon

 You're right: it was I gave you this
 because I knew from old days how you loved them
 as I see now.

Oedipus

      God bless you for it, Creon,
 and may God guard you better on your road
 than he did me!

O children, 1480
where are you? Come here, come to my hands,
a brother's hands which turned your father's eyes,
those bright eyes you knew once, to what you see,
a father seeing nothing, knowing nothing,
begetting you from his own source of life. 1485
I weep for you—I cannot see your faces—
I weep when I think of the bitterness
there will be in your lives, how you must live
before the world. At what assemblages
of citizens will you make one? to what 1490
gay company will you go and not come home
in tears instead of sharing in the holiday?
And when you're ripe for marriage, who will he be,
the man who'll risk to take such infamy
as shall cling to my children, to bring hurt 1495
on them and those that marry with them? What
curse is not there? "Your father killed his father
and sowed the seed where he had sprung himself
and begot you out of the womb that held him."
These insults you will hear. Then who will marry you? 1500
No one, my children; clearly you are doomed
to waste away in barrenness unmarried.
Son of Menoeceus, since you are all the father
left these two girls, and we, their parents, both 1505
are dead to them—do not allow them wander
like beggars, poor and husbandless.
They are of your own blood.
And do not make them equal with myself
in wretchedness; for you can see them now
so young, so utterly alone, save for you only.
Touch my hand, noble Creon, and say yes. 1510
If you were older, children, and were wiser,
there's much advice I'd give you. But as it is,
let this be what you pray: give me a life

wherever there is opportunity
to live, and better life than was my father's.

Creon

Your tears have had enough of scope; now go within the house.   1515

Oedipus

I must obey, though bitter of heart.

Creon

In season, all is good.

Oedipus

Do you know on what conditions I obey?

Creon

                    You tell me them,
and I shall know them when I hear.

Oedipus

                        That you shall send me out
to live away from Thebes.

Creon

                    That gift you must ask of the God.

Oedipus

But I'm now hated by the Gods.

Creon

                    So quickly you'll obtain your prayer.

Oedipus

You consent then?   1520

Creon

                    What I do not mean, I do not use to say.

Oedipus

Now lead me away from here.

Creon

                    Let go the children, then, and come.

Oedipus

Do not take them from me.

Creon
　　　　　Do not seek to be master in everything,
for the things you mastered did not follow you throughout your
　　life.

　　　　　　　　　　　(*As Creon and Oedipus go out.*)
Chorus
You that live in my ancestral Thebes, behold this Oedipus,—
him who knew the famous riddles and was a man most masterful;　1525
not a citizen who did not look with envy on his lot—
see him now and see the breakers of misfortune swallow him!
Look upon that last day always. Count no mortal happy till
he has passed the final limit of his life secure from pain.　　　1530

OEDIPUS AT COLONUS

CHARACTERS

Oedipus

Antigone

A Stranger

Ismene

Theseus

Creon

Polyneices

A Messenger

Chorus

OEDIPUS AT COLONUS

(Enter Oedipus, now a very old man, accompanied by
his daughter Antigone.)

Oedipus
 I am blind and old, Antigone, my child.
 What country have we come to? Whose is this city?
 Who will today receive the wandering
 Oedipus, with the scantiest of gifts?
 It's little I ask for, and still less I get,
 yet it is enough for me.
 My sufferings have taught me to endure—
 and how long these sufferings have lasted!—
 and my high breeding teaches me the same.

 Child, do you see anywhere I could sit,
 either on the common ground or in the groves   10
 belonging to the god? Set me there securely,
 that we may find out where we are; we have come to be learners
 as foreigners from citizens, to do as we are told.

Antigone
 My poor suffering father, Oedipus!
 there are towers here that protect the city; they look,
 to my eyes, far off. This place is sacred—
 as I would guess—it's thick with laurel,
 with olives and with vines; the nightingales are singing,
 thick-feathered, happily, inside the grove.
 Here's a rough rock; bend and sit down on it.
 This has been a long journey for an old man like you.   20

Oedipus
 Set me now in place, watch over the blind man.

Antigone

    I do not need to learn that now;
    time has seen to that.

Oedipus

    Can you tell me where we are?

Antigone

    Athens—that much I know—but not this place.

Oedipus

    Yes, Athens; every traveler has told us that.

Antigone

    Shall I go and try to find which this place is?

Oedipus

    Yes, child, if indeed there are people in it.

Antigone

    People there are; I think I need do nothing.
    I see a man now, near us.

Oedipus

    Are you sure? Is he really coming this way?   30

Antigone

    He is, indeed—here with us. Whatever you have
    that is suitable to say, say it; the man is here.

Oedipus

    Sir, I have heard her say—
    she has eyes for both of us—that you have come
    to inquire about us. Very opportunely
    you come to clear up our uncertainty.

Stranger

    Before you ask any more—up from this place
    where you are sitting! This is no ground to tread on.

Oedipus

    What is this place? What god is thought to possess it?

Stranger

It is inviolable, none may live in it. The Goddesses
most dreadful, the daughters of Earth and Darkness, possess it.   40

Oedipus

May I hear their sacred name to pray to them?

Stranger

The all-seeing Eumenides, the people here call them,
but they have other fair names elsewhere.

(A silence, broken by Oedipus' words.)

Oedipus

May they be gracious and receive their suppliant.
For I will never go from this land—from *this* place in it!

Stranger

What can you mean?

Oedipus

I have heard
the watchword of my destiny.

Stranger

No—I would certainly never have the boldness
to drive you out, without the city's sanction,
until I tell them what I am doing.

Oedipus

Sir, for God's sake, do not do me such dishonor—
poor wanderer that I am—to deny me
what I would beg you tell me.   50

Stranger

Then speak. I *shall* not do you such dishonor.

Oedipus

What *is* this place on which I have set foot?

Stranger

If you listen, I will tell you, whatever it is
I know myself. All of this place is sacred;

our holy lord Poseidon holds it. In it
there dwells Prometheus the Titan, fire-bearing god.
Within this land the spot you tread on
is the Bronze Road—so it is called—
it is the founding stone of Athens; the neighboring acres
boast that their ruler is the Knight Colonus
and all the people here bear his name in common.   60
That is how things are, sir; here is no mere honor in word;
the honor comes of living with the place, as theirs.

Oedipus

There are some, then, that live within this place?

Stranger

Yes, surely, those that are called by the god's name.

Oedipus

Have they a sovereign, or does the word rest with the people?

Stranger

They are ruled by the city's king.

Oedipus

                                                And who is he
that is so mighty both in power and word?

Stranger

His name is Theseus, son of Aegeus, that was.

Oedipus

Can a messenger go from you to him?   70

Stranger

                                        What for?
To tell him what, to urge his coming here?

Oedipus

That by small help he may reap great gains.

Stranger

Can a blind man give such help?

Oedipus

There shall be sight in all the words I say.

Stranger

    Let me tell you, sir, how you will make no mistake;
    You are noble—anyone can see that—in all but fortune.
    Remain here where I first saw you, until I go
    and tell my fellow citizens; not those in the city,
    but citizens of *this* place. They are those to judge
    whether you should stay here or again take the road.   80

Oedipus

    Child, is the stranger gone?

Antigone

                         Yes, he is gone;
    so, father, you may freely say everything,
    for only I am by.

       (Oedipus turns towards the grove and addresses those in it.)

Oedipus

    O solemn, dreadful-faced Ones,
    since first in this land with you I found my resting place
    and bent the knee there, be not unmindful
    of Phoebus and of me!
    For Phoebus when he prophesied those horrors,
    those many horrors for me, yet said that at the last
    I should find rest here, in this final country,
    when I should gain the haunt of the Dread Goddesses,
    a place of hospitality for strangers.   90
    There I should round my wretched life's last lap,
    a gain for those that settled me, received me,
    but a curse to those that drove me out.
    As warranty of this there should come signs,
    earthquakes and thunder, Zeus' lightning.
    Now I know well that I can trust your omen
    that guided me to this grove! Never, else, surely,
    had I in my traveling met with *you* first of all,
    I dry-mouthed, you that use no wine. Nor had I   100
    sat on this sacred undressed rock. But, Goddesses,

as Phoebus' mouth has spoken, give my life ending
at last, some consummation of my course,
unless I seem to you inconsequential,
a slave to toils, the greatest in the world.
Come, you sweet daughters of ancient Darkness,
come, city, called after great Pallas,
Athens, most full of honor of any city,
pity this wretched shade of the man Oedipus;
the body that once was Oedipus is no more.   110

Antigone

Hush! Here are some old men coming
to spy out where we are resting.

Oedipus

I will be silent.
Do you conceal me in the grove, out of the way,
till I can find out what they will say; if we only hear,
we can be cautious in our actions.

Chorus of old men, nobles of Athens

Look! Who was he? And where?
Where has he disappeared? Where has he hurried,
man of most impious daring? Look for him, search for him,   120
inquire everywhere! Some wandering tramp
he must be, not from hereabouts; else he had never
set foot within this sacred grove
of those violent virgins whom we tremble to name,
whose dwelling place we pass   130
with no eyes to look, and without voice to speak,
with silent guard on lips, that no words
may a pious mouth sound forth.

But now the story goes that someone has come
who shows no reverence at all,
and search as I may I cannot discover
who he may be.

Oedipus
   I am he; for I see
   by the sound of a voice, as the proverb runs.

Chorus
   Someone terrible to see,   140
   terrible to hear.

Oedipus
   Do not see me as a lawbreaker—
   that I entreat you.

Chorus
   Zeus the Defender, who can this old man be?

Oedipus
   Surely no one to congratulate
   on prime good fortune, guardians of this land.
   I can be clear on that; else others' eyes
   would not so guide my erring steps,
   else had my greatness not found its anchor
   on those that are but little.

Chorus
   Woe for your blinded eyes! Were you so from birth?   150
   Old and unfortunate
   is how you look to us.
   But at least if it lies with me,
   you should not add another curse on yourself.
   You advance too far, too far! Take heed
   lest you stumble on that grassy stretch
   where the mixing bowl
   mixes its water with the stream that runs
   sweetened with honey.   160
   Unlucky stranger, watch heedfully. Away!
   Step right away! He is too far away to hear!
   Do you hear, you sorrowful wanderer?

If you want to speak and answer us,
leave that forbidden place and speak
where all may speak. Till then be silent.

Oedipus
Daughter, what should one think of this?   170

Antigone
Father, we must do as other citizens here,
yielding in what is dutiful, hearing with obedience.

Oedipus
Reach out your hand to me.

Antigone
Here do I reach it out.

Oedipus
Sirs, let me not meet with injustice
now I have trusted you and moved my ground.

Chorus
Old man, no one shall lead you
against your will, from where you rest at present.

Oedipus
Must I go further still?

Chorus
Still further.

Oedipus
Still further?

Chorus
Lead him, girl,   180
somewhat further. *You* are listening to me.

[*R. C. Jebb, the main English commentator on Sophocles, thinks
that here there are three lines lost, in interchanges between Oedipus and
Antigone.*]

Antigone
> Follow me then, follow me
> with your blind steps; follow where I lead you.

[Jebb thinks that a line is lost here also.]

Chorus
> You are a stranger in a strange land,
> poor man. Make your mind up
> to reject what this city dislikes,
> and reverence what she loves.

Oedipus
> Lead me on, child,
> to where, my feet once more on pious footing,
> I may speak and hear.   190
> We must not fight against necessity.

Chorus
> Here, do not bend your steps
> beyond this block of natural stone.

Oedipus
> Is this as you want it?

Chorus
> Far enough, I tell you.

Oedipus
> May I sit?

Chorus
> Yes, sideways, on the edge of the rock,
> crouch low.

Antigone
> Father, let me help you—this is my task—   200
> step evenly with me.
> Lean your old body on my arm that loves it.

(Oedipus groans.)

Oedipus
  Oh, for the mischief that haunts my mind!

Chorus
  Poor man, now that you rest,
  tell me—who are you?
  Who are you that is led so sorrowfully?
  May we ask what is your country?

Oedipus
  Sirs, I have no city; please do not—

Chorus
  Do not do what, old man?

Oedipus
  Do not ask who I am; do not push further   210
  in your inquiry.

Chorus
  Why so?

Oedipus
  My breeding is full of terror.

Chorus
  Tell me.

Oedipus
  Daughter, what am I to say?

                                        (He breaks into a sob.)

Chorus
  Tell me what stock you are of, sir, and your father.

Oedipus (sobbing)
  What will become of me, child?

Antigone
  Tell them. You are as far as you can go.

Oedipus
  I will tell them, then. Indeed, I cannot hide it.

Chorus
You are slow and hesitant. Be quick and tell us.

Oedipus
Do you know a son
of Laius?

220

Chorus
Oh, yes, yes!

Oedipus
He was of the family of the Labdacids.

Chorus
O Zeus!

Oedipus
The miserable Oedipus.

Chorus
And you are *he*?

Oedipus
Do not be so terrified
at what I say.

Chorus
(*cries out*)

Oedipus
A doomed man.

Chorus
(*cries out*)

Oedipus
Daughter,
what will become of me *now*?

Chorus
Out of this place, out of it!

Oedipus

And your promise? What will that be?

Chorus

Punishment is not the due lot of anyone
who but requites what is already done to him.   230
Trickery matching others' trickery gives
pain and not pleasure in return.
Up from this place!—and from this country where
you have found an anchorage!
Do not fix upon my city
some further debt to bear.

Antigone

Sirs, you have honor in your hearts,
but you cannot bear with my father, old and blind,
because you have heard the tale
of acts done in unconsciousness!   240
Yet, sirs, take pity on my wretched self;
I who beg you for my father only.
I beg you, with eyes not blinded, facing your eyes,
as though I came of your own blood,
that he, in his unhappiness, win your mercy.
What happens to us lies in your hands,
as though you were a god.
Come, grant me a favor—though I scarce look for it—
I entreat you by all that is dear to you—   250
by child or wife, by duty or by god.
No matter where you look, you will find no man
who can escape if a god leads him on.

Chorus

Why, know, you child of Oedipus, that you and he
both win our pity for your calamity.
But we dread judgment from the gods. We cannot
say more than what we have said to you already.

Oedipus

What is the good of a glorious reputation

if it is like an idly flowing stream?
They say that Athens is the holiest of cities,   260
say that she always rescues the injured stranger,
that she alone is able to defend him.
Where are these things for me? You moved me out
from the safety of this rock; then drive me out
forth from your country—fearing my name alone!
Surely not what I am nor what I have done.
Indeed, what I have done
is suffering rather than doing, if I were to tell you
the story of both my parents, which makes you dread me.
That I know well. How can my nature be evil,   270
when all I did was matching others' actions?
Even had I done what I did full consciously,
even so, I would not have been evil.
But the truth is, I knew nothing
when I came where I did. Yet *they* knew—
those by whom I suffered—knew what they did.
It was meant to be my death.
Therefore, sirs, I beseech you by the gods,
since you took me from my place of safety, save me now.
Do not, as honoring the gods, fail to give those gods
their dues of recognition. Think that they look
upon those that respect the gods and those
who do not so—among all men in the world.   280
Never yet has the wicked man got clear away,
escaping them. Take the side of those gods, do not dim the glory
of Athens by serving deeds of wickedness.
Rescue me, guard me; do not see the ugliness
of my face to its dishonor.
I am here as sacred and pious both,
and bringing benefit to your citizens.
When your lord comes here—whoever is your leader—
you shall hear all and understand it all.
In the time between these words and his arrival   290
do not turn villains.

Chorus

    We needs must fear, old man, those haunted thoughts
    coming from you; the words that clothe them are not light.
    It is enough for me that this land's princes
    shall know the matter through and through.

Oedipus

    Sirs, where is the ruler of this land?

Chorus

    He is in his father's city, in our country.
    The man who sent me here has gone to fetch him.

Oedipus

    Do you believe that he will care so much
    to give a thought to a blind man—that he will come
    himself to see me?   300

Chorus

    He surely will when he has heard your name.

Oedipus

    Who is there that will bring *that* word to him?

Chorus

    It is a long road here; there are many travelers
    and many tales of theirs; these he will hear
    and come; do not trouble for that. Your name, old man,
    has pierced the ears of many; were he asleep
    or slow to move, yet when he hears
    of *you,* he will come quickly to this place.

Oedipus

    Well, may he come, with good luck for this city,
    and for me, too! For what good man is there
    who is no friend to himself?

Antigone

    Zeus, what shall I say? What am I to think, father?   310

Oedipus

    What is it, Antigone, my child?

Antigone
>I see a girl
>coming towards us riding an Etnean horse;
>on her head is a Thessalian bonnet
>which shields her from the sun. What do I say?
>Is it really she? or not? does my mind cheat me?
>It is—it isn't—I cannot tell—
>It *is* she and no other. Her eyes are all aglow
>as she comes to welcome me. That shows it is she—   320
>she and no other, Ismene, my darling!

Oedipus
>What is it you say, child?

Antigone
>That I see your daughter,
>my own sister. Soon you will know,
>hearing her voice.

Ismene
>Dear father and sister—how sweet are both those names!
>How hard it was to find you, and now you are found,
>how hard, again, to see you, for my tears!

Oedipus
>You have really come, my child?

Ismene
>Father—how hard to see you so!

Oedipus
>You are really there, child!

Ismene
>Yes, though it was hard to come here.

Oedipus
>Touch me, my child.

Ismene
>I touch you both alike.

Oedipus
  Sisters. True sisters both!

Ismene
  How wretched this life of ours.   330

Oedipus
  You mean, her life and mine?

Ismene
  Yes, and mine too.

Oedipus
  Why have you come?

Ismene
  Through care of you.

Oedipus
  Because you longed to see me?

Ismene
  Yes, and to tell you things
  with my own tongue. My companion here
  was the only trusty servant that I have.

Oedipus
  Where are those brothers of your blood
  to do us service now?

Ismene
  They are where they are.
  This is a terrible time for them.

Oedipus
  Those two are like in everything
  to the ways of Egypt,
  both in their nature and in how they live.
  For in that country the men sit within doors
  working at the loom, while the wives go out   340
  to get the daily bread.
  So, children, those two brothers of yours, who should

bear the stress and strain, keep house within, like girls,
and you, in their stead, struggle to bear my troubles.
You, Antigone, since you ceased to be a child,
and had grown strong enough, wandered with me always,
to your unhappiness, guiding an old man's steps.
Many a time you strayed in the wild woods,
without a bite to eat and barefoot;
many a wet day, many a burning sunlight   350
you toiled through; you never thought
of home or comfort in comparison
with the need to earn your father the means to live.
And you, Ismene, in the old time came to me
unknown to the Cadmeans, with all their oracles
that spoke about this carcass of mine.
You were my trusty guard when I was hunted
out of Theban land.
But now again what tale have you to tell me,
your father? What mission started you from your home?
I am very sure you are not empty-handed,
but carry with you some terror affecting me.   360

Ismene

What I endured in looking for you, father—
in trying to find where you were living—
let me leave alone. I do not want to suffer
twice over, in the doing and telling both.
But I have come here to declare to you
the evils that befell your unhappy sons.

At first their passionate wish—as it was Creon's—
was to leave the throne to him, and not pollute
the city further. They looked sensibly
at the old destruction that lay on their breeding,
which indeed beset your unlucky house.   370
But now stirred by some god
and by some sinfulness of mind themselves,

a deadly spirit of competition
has entered these thrice unhappy beings
to grasp the government and the monarchy;
and the younger born, his hot blood up,
would rob his elder brother Polyneices
of the throne and has banished him the country.
The elder, as rumor multiplied declares,
went into exile in hollow Argos,
and there took to himself a new marriage tie
and for new friends new fellow spearmen,
his aim that Argos should possess in honor   380
the land of Thebes or else exalt to heaven
the Theban power by the defeat of Argos.
This is no empty sum of words, my father;
they are deeds and terrible. At what point the gods
will pity your tribulations I cannot guess.

Oedipus
  Did you really hope the gods would take any heed
  of me, enough some day to rescue me?

Ismene
  I do, my father, from these present oracles.

Oedipus
  And what are they? What has been prophesied,
  my child?

Ismene
  That you shall one day be desired
  by Thebes, yes, living and dead you *shall* be,
  for their own welfare's sake.   390

Oedipus
  How can anyone's welfare depend
  on such as I am?

Ismene
  With you, they say, there rests
  their victory.

Oedipus
>When I *am* no longer
>then am I a man?

Ismene
>Yes, father, for today the gods exalt you;
>then they destroyed you.

Oedipus
>It is a poor thing to exalt the old
>when he fell in his youth.

Ismene
>Still, you must know that Creon
>for these very causes is coming here,
>and shortly, without loss of time.

Oedipus
>What would he do,
>my daughter? Explain that to me.

Ismene
>They want to place you near the land of Thebes,
>to own you, still not letting your foot tread
>within the borders of their country.   400

Oedipus
>What good can I do, lying outside their doors?

Ismene
>The place you lie in—if it suffer wrong—
>will be a heavy curse on them.

Oedipus
>One needs no god to have the knowledge of that.

Ismene
>Well, that is why they want to have you as an ally,
>near to their land, but not as your own master.

Oedipus
>Will they let the shadowing dust of Thebes lie on me?

Ismene

No, for the guilt of family bloodletting
debars it, father.

Oedipus

Then they will never own me.

Ismene

So shall there be a heavy weight of sorrow
upon the Thebans.

Oedipus

In what conjunction, child, shall this come to pass?   410

Ismene

When your anger strikes them, as they stand on your grave.

Oedipus

What you say now—from whom did you hear that?

Ismene

The sacred envoys when they came back from Delphi.

Oedipus

And that was, truly, what Phoebus said about me?

Ismene

So the men said that came to Thebes from Delphi.

Oedipus

Did either of my sons know this about me?

Ismene

Both of them equally; both knew it well.

Oedipus

And then those villains, when they heard of it,
longed for me less than for this throne of theirs?

Ismene

I hate to hear that said, but I must bear it.   420

Oedipus

Then may the gods never quench their fated quarrel
and may it lie in *my* hands to determine

the end of the fight, which now they seek so eagerly
with their raised spears. If that shall happen
neither he that presently holds throne and scepter
shall remain where he is; nor he the exile
shall return home. I am their father
and when I was dishonored and driven out
from my own land, they never hindered it,
nor helped defend me; as far as they could do it,
it was those two expelled me; by them I was proclaimed exile.   430
You might say that *then* I also willed it so,
and that the city granted me that gift.
This is not so; for on the day itself
when my spirit seethed, and death was dearest to me,
yes, death by stoning, no one would help me to it.
But when time had gone by,
and all the agony had mellowed,
when I felt my agony had outrun itself
in punishing my former sins—it was then and then   440
the city drove me out—after all that time!—
in my despite—and these, these sons of mine,
could have helped me, their father, but they would not.
No, for the lack of one short word from them
I was banished, a beggar, to wander forever.
But it was from *these,* girls as they are,
as far as their nature could, I had my sustenance,
and ground to tread on without fear,
and the support of kinfolk.
Those other two, above their father's claims·
chose sovereignty, wielding the scepter,
and their land's lordship. No, they will never win me   450
to be their ally, nor shall there ever come
profit to them from their reign in Thebes:
that I know well, both from Ismene's oracles,
which I now hear, and when I recollect
those of old days which Phoebus has accomplished
now in this time.

So let them send Creon to fetch me in,
or anyone else of power within their city,
for if you, my foreign friends, are willing,
backed by those solemn goddesses
that are your champions, to grant me your protection,
you will win for your city
a mighty service and for enemies, trouble.   460

Chorus

Oedipus, you certainly deserve pity,
yourself and your daughters; and since you add to the count
that you will be the savior of our country,
may I suggest to you thoughts perhaps useful?

Oedipus

Dear friend: do but be my champion,
and be assured I will do all you tell me.

Chorus

Make an atonement to those deities
you came to first, when you trespassed on their ground.

Oedipus

In what fashion shall I do it? Tell me, sirs.

Chorus

First bring a sacred draught from the everlasting
springs there; and let the hands that bring it be pure.   470

Oedipus

And when I take this draught unsullied—what then?

Chorus

There are bowls there, work of a skillful maker;
crown the top of each, and the handles at either side.

Oedipus

With twigs or flocks of wool—or how shall I do it?

Chorus

With a flock of wool, new shorn, from a ewe lamb.

Oedipus
Very well; after that what must I do?

Chorus
Pour your offerings, with your face towards the first dawn.

Oedipus
Shall I pour them from the vessels that you speak of?

Chorus
Yes, in three streams; the last must empty the bowl.

Oedipus
What shall I fill the third with before I set it?
Tell me that, too.   480

Chorus
With water and with honey.
Do not bring wine near it.

Oedipus
And when the dark-shading earth has drunk of it?

Chorus
Then with both hands, taking nine sprigs of olive,
lay them on it; and say this prayer over them.

Oedipus
That I would hear—that is the greatest thing!

Chorus
"As we call these the Kindly Ones, with kindly
hearts may they welcome this suppliant for his saving."
So pray, or those who speak for you.
But say the words inaudibly; do not raise your voice.
Then go away—and do not look behind you.
If you do this, I will stand by your side and welcome.   490
Otherwise, sir, I will fear on your behalf.

Oedipus
My children, you have heard the strangers who live here?

Antigone
We have heard; do you but tell us what to do.

Oedipus

    I cannot go myself; I fail in strength
    and sight, my double weakness.
    One of you must go and do this thing,
    for I think that one soul—be it but a well-wisher's—
    can pay the debt for tens of thousands.
    Quickly now; but do not leave me alone.   500
    My body cannot move, lonely of help,
    nor without guidance.

Ismene

    I will go to do it.
    But I must know where I should find the place.

Chorus

    On the other side of the grove, girl. If you need anything,
    a man lives there who will tell you.

Ismene

    I will go to my task; Antigone,
    stay here and guard our father; for a parent's sake,
    whatever trouble there is—if there is any—
    does not count.

Chorus

    It is a dreadful thing, sir,   510
    to awaken again an old ill that lies quiet.
    Yet still I long to know—

Oedipus

    What? What do you mean?

Chorus

    Of the pain that besets your life,
    so remediless, so wretched—

Oedipus

    Do not, I beg you—
    I am your guest; you were kind to me.
    Do not lay bare my sufferings;
    they are beyond shame.

Chorus
It is a story that has spread far;
it doesn't die out. I would like to hear the right of it.

Oedipus
(moans)

Chorus
Endure the pain, I say.

Oedipus
Oh, oh.

Chorus
Do as I beg you. I gave you what *you* asked.   520

Oedipus
I bore the worst of sufferings—but for deeds—
be God my witness!—done without knowledge.
In all this there was nothing of conscious choice.

Chorus
How was it?

Oedipus
It was the city bound me,
in utter ignorance, in a deadly marriage,
in fated ruin, that came with my wife.

Chorus
Was it then, as I hear,
that you filled your bed
with your mother to your infamy?

Oedipus
Oh, it is death to hear it said,
strangers. These two girls of mine—   530

Chorus
You mean—

Oedipus
Yes, my children, they are the two
curses upon me.

Chorus
Zeus!

Oedipus
They sprang from the womb that bore me also.

Chorus
Then they are your children and—

Oedipus
Their father's sisters, too.

[*The passage that follows is difficult to understand. The Chorus has from the first, on hearing Oedipus' name, seemed to know the story. Apparently this may not be the case—at least the story in its entirety. There is another version of the myth, a fragment of Theban epic known to Pausanias, the very much later author of the geography of Greece, according to which the children of Oedipus here, Ismene and Antigone, are the children of his second wife, Euryganeia. Odyssey XI 271 is not explicit on this, but there are other aspects of its difference from our version—e.g., after Jocasta killed herself, Oedipus went on ruling Thebes. R. C. Jebb thinks it was the Attic dramatists who first introduced into the story the bearing of the incest on the daughters (Jebb, Commentary on O.C. 534). If this is right, the Chorus in the passage following this does make a genuinely new discovery from Oedipus. They may have been following till then the other and older version of the myth. The half lines of each speaker, each completing the statement, is far from anything we find dramatic. The whole is written in semi-lyrical meters and was probably delivered in a semi-ritualized manner, a kind of singsong interchange, almost like a dirge. It is of course extremely difficult for a translator to render tolerably.*]

Chorus
Oh, oh!

Oedipus
Ten thousand horrors sweep back upon me.

Chorus
You have suffered—

Oedipus

What I can never forget.

Chorus
But you *did*—

Oedipus

I *did* nothing.

Chorus
How can that be?

Oedipus

I received a gift
for serving the city—would to God I had never won it!—   540
for my heart is broken.

Chorus
Unhappy man! But you did a murder.

Oedipus
How a murder? What is it you would know?

Chorus
Your father's murder.

Oedipus
You strike me again, wound upon wound.

Chorus
But you killed him.

Oedipus
Yes, I killed him, but he had from me—

Chorus
What?

Oedipus
Something of justice.

Chorus
How can that be?

Oedipus

I will tell you.
Those that I killed would have killed me.
So in law I am innocent and came to all this
in ignorance.

Chorus

Here is our king, Theseus, son of Aegeus,
to do what the news of you summoned him to do.   550

Theseus

In time past, son of Laius, I have heard from many
of the bloody blinding of your eyes—and I recognized you.
Now as I heard more on my journey here
I am in greater certainty.
The clothes you wear and your unhappy face
show us clearly who you are. Because you have
my pity, unfortunate Oedipus, I would ask you
what is this supplication you urge on Athens
and on myself—you and the poor girl beside you?
Tell me. You must tell me something dreadful indeed   560
to make me turn away from you.
For my part I know what it means,
myself, to be brought up in exile,
as you are in exile. I too in a foreign country
wrestled with dangers to my life, more than anyone else.
So there is surely no stranger, such as you,
from whom I would turn my face, nor help to save.
For I am very certain I am but a man:
as such, I have of tomorrow no greater share
than you have.

Oedipus

Theseus, your nobleness in one short speech
has left me the necessity of saying little.   570
You have said about me all that is true—
who I am, from what father born, from what country come.

All that is left me to say is what I want,
and then the story is told.

Theseus
Tell me; let me know.

Oedipus
I come to give you this wretched carcass of mine,
a gift to you; to look at, no great matter,
but no beautiful body will give you such gains as it will.

Theseus
What is this gain you claim to bring with you?

Oedipus
In time you will know—but the time is not yet, I think.   580

Theseus
When will your benefit be shown?

Oedipus
When I die and you shall have been my burial man.

Theseus
You ask about the last moments of your life;
what lies between this and then
you either forget or have no heed of.

Oedipus
Yes:
when that is given, my whole harvest is in.

Theseus
The favor you ask me lies in small compass, then?

Oedipus
Watch that; it is no easy fight to win.

Theseus
Do you mean between your sons and me?

Oedipus
Yes.
They wish to carry me away to Thebes.

Theseus

    Well, if you are willing— 590
    exile is not a fine thing.

Oedipus

    When I myself was willing they would not let me.

Theseus

    You are being foolish; anger does not sit well
    with folk in trouble.

Oedipus

    Rebuke me when you understand, and not till then.

Theseus

    Then tell me. True, without knowledge I should not speak.

Oedipus

    I have suffered, Theseus, terribly, evils upon evils.

Theseus

    You mean what befell your family from of old?

Oedipus

    No. That is the talk of everyone in Greece.

Theseus

    What then is your suffering beyond all men's endurance?

Oedipus

    This is how it is. I was banished from my own country
    by my own sons, return forever denied me, 600
    because I killed my father.

Theseus

    How then would they send for you
    if it is but to settle you apart?

Oedipus

    It is the mouth of God will force them to it.

Theseus

    What is it, then, they fear foretold in oracles?

Oedipus

That they must be smitten by this land of yours.

Theseus

But how should there be bitterness between
them and myself?

Oedipus

O dearest son of Aegeus:
only the gods know neither age nor death;
everything else all-mastering time confounds.
The strength of earth, the strength of body, dies;   610
trust dies, distrust comes into blossoming.
The same breath does not blow from man to man,
constant in friendship, nor in city towards city.
It may be now, it may be later, sometime
the sweet turns bitter, and then again to friendship.
If now the day is bright betwixt you and Thebes,
uncounted time in course will breed uncounted
nights and days, shattering with the spear
those right hands presently clasped in harmony.
The cause will be so slight!   620
At that time my body hidden in earth and sleeping
will coldly drink their hot blood,
if Zeus be still Zeus and if Zeus' son
Phoebus speak clearly.
But it is not pleasant
to speak the words that should lie undisturbed.
Let me stop where I began; do you only keep
the pledge you gave me and you will never say
that you received as dweller in this land,
a worthless fellow, Oedipus—
unless the gods shall cheat me.

Chorus

My lord, this man has talked like this before,
as though he would do something for our country.   630

Theseus

 Who would reject goodwill in such a man?
 In the first place, forever a hearth between us
 speaks of guest-friendship and a spear alliance.
 And then he has come a suppliant of these Goddesses,
 and promises to this land and myself
 no inconsiderable recompense.
 These matters claim my reverence and so
 I will not reject his claim upon my gratitude.
 I will make him our citizen. If it be his pleasure,
 this stranger's, to remain here I will charge you
 to guard him. (*Turning to Oedipus.*)
     Or, if you please to come with me,
 Oedipus, I submit to your judgment.   640
 It shall be as you choose.

Oedipus

 May God send blessings on such men as you!

Theseus

 What would you, then? Will you come to my home?

Oedipus

 I would—if it were lawful. But this place here—

Theseus

 What would you do in "this place"? I will not oppose you.

Oedipus

 It is *here* I will conquer those that cast me out.

Theseus

 This would be a great gift of your staying here.

Oedipus

 If you stand fast by what you said and do it.

Theseus

 You need not fear for me. I will not fail you.

Oedipus

 I will not put you on your oath like someone base.   650

Theseus
No oath will give you more than my bare word.

Oedipus
What will you do then—

Theseus
                    What is it you fear most?

Oedipus
Some will come here—

Theseus
                    My friends will take care of *that*.

Oedipus
See you do not fail me—

Theseus
                    Do not tell me my duty.

Oedipus
It is inevitable that I should fear.

Theseus
                             I do not fear.

Oedipus
You do not know the threats—

Theseus
                    I do know that no one
will take you out of here against my will.
There are many threats, and many threatening words
issue out of anger. When the mind is master of itself,
the threats have vanished.   660
Perhaps these people had strength enough to speak
dreadful things of your carrying off, but *I* know
the sea to sail between us will seem long,
poor prospects for a voyage. I would say to you
"Be of good cheer" even without my judgment,
since Phoebus sent you hither. Even though *I* were not here,
my *name* will guard you against ill-usage.

Chorus

Here are the fairest homesteads of the world,
here in this country, famed for its horses, stranger,
where you have come:
Here to Colonus, gleaming white,   670
where the nightingale in constant trilling song
cries from beneath the green leaves,
where she lives in the wine dark ivy
and the dark foliage of ten thousand berries,
safe from the sun, safe from the wind
of every storm, god's place, inviolable.
Where Dionysus the reveler paces
thronged by the nymphs his nurses.   680

Here there blooms, fed by heaven's dew,
daily and ever, the lovely-clustered narcissus,
the ancient crown of the Great Goddesses,
and also the golden gleaming crocus.
Nor fail the wandering springs
that feed the streams of Cephisus,
but daily and ever the river
with his pure waters gives increase
over the swelling bosom of the land.   690
This country the bands of the Muses
have not disdained
nor yet Aphrodite of the Golden Reins.
There is a thing too, of which no other like
I have heard in Asian land,
nor as ever grown in the great Dorian
island of Pelops,
a plant unconquered and self-renewing,
a terror that strikes the spear-armed enemy,
a plant that flourishes greatest here,   700
leaf of gray olive,
nourishing our children.

It shall not be rendered impotent
by the young nor by him that lives with old age,
destroying it with violence,
for the ever-living eye of Morian Zeus
looks upon it—and gray-eyed Athene also.

Yet another matter of praise have I
for this my mother city,
gift of a great god, our land's great boast,   710
that it is horse master, colt breaker, master of the sea.
Son of Cronus, Lord Poseidon,
you it is who have set her in that glory.
For you are the one who in these roads first
established the bit to control the horse,
and the oar, too, well fitted to the hand
leaps marvelously in the sea,
following the hundred-footed Nereids.

Antigone
  Land with praises richly celebrated,   720
  now be it yours to make those praises shine.

Oedipus
  What is there new, child?

Antigone
  Creon draws near.
  Here he is—and with followers.

Oedipus (to the Chorus)
  Old men,
  my friends, now manifest, I beg you,
  the last goal of my safety.

Chorus
  Courage!
  That safety shall be yours. If *I* am old,
  the strength of Attica has not grown old.

Creon

    Sirs, noble gentlemen of this land,
    I see your eyes have suddenly taken fright
    at my intrusion. I beg you, do not fear   730
    nor speak ill words to me.
    I have come with no determination
    to offer any violence. I am old myself
    and know I have come to a city powerful
    as any is in Greece.
    I was sent, old as I am, to urge this man
    to come with me to Thebes.
    No single person sent me. I have my orders
    from the whole commonality. They sent *me*
    because it was I who was most concerned
    (because of our relationship) to sorrow,
    most of all within our city, for *his* troubles.

    Unhappy Oedipus, hear me and come home!   740
    All the Cadmean people summon you, and rightly,
    and most of all do I, in the proportion
    that I must be the worst of scoundrels
    if I felt no pain at these your sufferings.
    I see you an unfortunate wretch, a foreigner,
    a beggar always and your sightless journeyings
    propped on this one girl only. I could not believe
    that she could fall to such a depth of misery
    as this unhappy child here, tending you
    and your life in daily beggary, young as she is,   750
    but with no part in marriage, a ready victim
    to be seized and raped by anyone.
    It *is* a miserable reproach, is it not?,
    that I have cast on you—and on me and all our breed.
    There is no hiding it. It's plain.
    But, Oedipus, it is you—I beg you—by our fathers' gods, *you,*
    listen to my words! it is *you* should hide it,
    by willingness to come to your own city

and to the house that was your fathers'.
Greet this city kindly—of course she has deserved it!—
but your own country should be honored more,
in justice, for she bred you up at first.   760

Oedipus
You would dare anything; from every plea of justice
you can extract some means of trickery.
Why do you try so? Why do you want
to catch me once again, when the catching will hurt most?
In the old time I was so sick in my troubles
that it had been my pleasure to be exiled;
but then when I was willing, you were not
to give me any such favor. But when my anger
was sated of itself, when living in that house
had become sweet to me, you threw me out,
you banished me. In that day this kinship you speak of   770
was no way dear to you.
And now again, when you see this city friendly
to my staying, when you see all the people friendly,
you try to tear me out, the harshness of your message
so softly rendered!
Yet, what pleasure can you have in showing kindness
to those that will not welcome it? It is as if
one begged for something, but was given nothing,
nor was there wish to help; but when the spirit
was sated with what one had sought for, then only,
one got the gift, when the grace carried no grace.
Surely this is an empty pleasure you gain.   780
And that indeed is what you have given me,
where the words are good and the substance evil.
I will show these people what a villain you are.
You have come to bring me, yes, but *not* to bring me home
but to set me in a dwelling apart—but near you,
so there will be no trouble with Athens for your city.
You will not succeed, no, instead

my spirit shall dwell forever, a curse,
a curse upon your country.
For these sons of mine, this is my prayer—
so much of their father's earth as to make their graves.   790
Am I not wiser than you in Theban matters?
Far wiser, for I learn from clearer speakers,
Phoebus and Zeus himself, that is his father.
But you have come here, a mouth suborned,
but with a right sharp tongue. For all that, in your speaking
you will win more harm than safety.
However, I know I am not persuading you.
Get gone!
Let us live here; even as it is
we would live well enough
if we are content.

Creon
    Who do you think has had the worst of it   800
    in this discussion? I in respect to you
    or you towards yourself?

Oedipus
    What I find most pleasant is your failure
    to persuade me or these men here.

Creon
    You miserable creature, clearly you haven't
    been able to grow wise, with all your years.

Oedipus
    You have a clever tongue, but I never knew a just man
    speak equally well on every plea.

Creon
    Saying much is one thing, seasonableness another.

Oedipus
    As though *your* words were few but very seasonable!

Creon

    Not seasonable, of course, for one so clever   810
    as you are.

Oedipus

    Away with you! I will speak on these men's behalf;
    do not watch and hem me in; this is where I live.

Creon

    I call these men to witness, not you, for what you have answered
    to those of us who are your family. If ever I catch you—

Oedipus

    How will you catch me in despite of these allies?

Creon

    I can hurt you enough without such action.

Oedipus

    What lies behind these threats of yours?

Creon

                             You have
    two daughters, one of whom I have seized
    and sent away. The other I will take soon.

Oedipus

    O God!

Creon

    Soon you will have more reason to cry out.   820

Oedipus

    You have my child?

Creon

                   And will have *this* one soon.

Oedipus

    Sirs, what will you do? Will you betray your trust?
    Will you not get rid of this unholy wretch?

Chorus
> Here, you, sir, off with you! What you are doing
> is utterly unjust. So is what you *have* done.

Creon (to his servants)
> It is high time for you to lead her off.
> If she won't go willingly, force her!

Antigone
> What refuge have I? What help can I find
> from god or man?

Chorus
>   What are you about, sir?

Creon
> I will not take the man, but *she* is mine.   830

Oedipus
> O, princes of this country!

Chorus
>   Sir, this is injustice!

Creon
> No, it is just.

Chorus
> How can it be just?

Creon
> I take my own.

Oedipus
> O city of Athens!

Chorus
> What are you doing, sir? Release her at once.
> If not—a trial of strength between us!

Creon
> Give way!

Chorus
>   Not to you while this is your purpose.

Creon
  You will fight with Thebes, if you do me an injury.

Oedipus
  Did I not say
  this is how it would be?

Chorus
  Release that girl at once.

Creon
                              Do not give orders
  that you cannot enforce.

Chorus
  I tell you take your hands off her!

Creon
                                              I tell you
  take a walk!   840

Chorus
  Come, countrymen of ours, come here, come here!
  The city is made nothing of, our city,
  by this violence. Come here, come here to us!

Antigone
  Friends, I am dragged away.

Oedipus
                              Where are you, child?

Antigone
  They are forcing me away!

Oedipus
  Reach me your hands!

Antigone
  I cannot I cannot.

Creon (to the servants)
  Bring her away, you!

Oedipus
> O God, O God!

Creon
> Well, on these crutches you will not travel again.
> But since you are determined to beat your country,
> and your family at whose command I do   850
> what I do—although I am their sovereign lord as well—
> enjoy your victory. In time you will know,
> I am certain, that what you do to yourself at present
> is nothing good, nor what you did before,
> when in the teeth of your friends you yielded to temper.
> It is your temper which constantly ruins you.

Chorus
> Stop right there, sir.

Creon
>   I warn you, do not touch me.

Chorus
> Give back the girls. Else you will not go from here.

Creon
> You will soon give my city a greater prize
> for our security. I will take more than these.

Chorus
> What will you do next?

Creon
>   I will take and carry *him* off.   860

Chorus
> An outrageous threat!

Creon
> It shall be executed.

Chorus
> Unless this country's ruler thwarts you.

Oedipus
> A shameless thing to say! Will you seize me indeed?

Creon

Hold your tongue!

Oedipus

May the gods of this place
not take away my tongue from uttering this curse!
You villain: after the violence to my onetime eyes,
you have wrenched from me the one poor eye I had left.
May the Sun-God that sees all give you and your seed
an old age like this of mine!   870

Creon

Do you see that, you people of this country?

Oedipus

They see both you and me; they understand
I am wronged in deeds, my defense, words only.

Creon

I'll not hold back my anger. I will bring him away by force,
although I am alone and slow with age.

Oedipus

(*cries out*)

Chorus

You have a bold spirit, sir, to think to come here,
and do as you do.

Creon

Yes, I believe I have.

Chorus

If you are right, I will no longer think
Athens a city.

Creon

With a just cause the weak subdue the strong.   880

Oedipus

Do you hear what he says?

Chorus
> But he will not act it—
> Zeus knows!

Creon
>   Zeus maybe knows—not you.

Chorus
> The insolence of this!

Creon
> Insolence you must put up with.

Chorus
> You people, and the rulers of this state, come here to us!
> Come quickly. These men will cross the border.

>   *(Theseus enters.)*

Theseus
> What is this noise about? What has happened here?
> You have stopped me in my sacrifice to the sea-god,
> lord of Colonus here: I was at the altar.
> What fear made you do that? Tell me. I want
> to know it all, why I have been made to hasten
> faster than I liked to this place here.   890

Oedipus
> Dearest of men, I recognize your voice. I have suffered
> dreadfully, right now, at this man's hands.

Theseus
> What happened? Who has injured you? Speak!

Oedipus
> Creon here, before your eyes, has taken my two
> children, all that I had.

Theseus
> What is this you say?

Oedipus
> You have heard what he did to me.

Theseus (points to his servants)
> Here, quickly, one of you go to the altars,
> urge all the people to leave the sacrifice
> and hurry, on horseback and on foot,
> at a full gallop to that place hereabouts   900
> where the two traveled roads combine,
> so that the girls won't get across and I,
> worsted by violence, become a mockery
> to my guest-friend.
> Away you go! Quickly! As I told you.
> For you, Creon, if I went as far in anger
> as you deserve, you would not go without
> marks of my hands upon you.
> However, such laws as he imported here
> shall be made to fit him—these and no others.

(He speaks directly to Creon.)

> You shall not leave this country until you bring here
> these girls for me to see. What you have done   910
> is a disgrace to me, and your own blood,
> and to your country. You came within this city
> that makes a practice of justice and determines
> nothing without a law. You then throw aside
> her lawful institutions by your invasion.
> You take what you want, making them yours by force.
> Apparently you thought this city quite unmanned
> or some slave place, and me a nobody.
> Yet it is not Thebes has taught you to be so bad.
> They do not usually rear men as wrongdoers,   920
> nor would the Thebans praise you if they heard
> you had violated what are mine and the gods' possessions,
> dragging out the helpless creatures that are their suppliants.
> I certainly never would have put foot on your soil—

not if I had the justest cause in the world—
without permission of the governors, whoever.
I would not have harried and plundered; I would have known
how I ought—a foreigner among citizens—
to conduct myself. But you dishonor
a city that has not merited dishonor—
your own city; and your years, so many,   930
show you an old man still empty of wisdom.
So I tell you now what I have said before;
let someone bring those girls here—quickly, too—
unless you want to be a resident alien
of Athens, under constraint, not voluntarily.
That is what I have to say. It comes from my full meaning,
not simply from my tongue.

Chorus
    You see what you have come to, sir. You appear
    to be of those who are just, but what you do
    is found to be evil.

Creon
    Of course I did not think this city unmanned,
    son of Aegeus, nor yet without wisdom as you claim,   940
    when I did this thing I did. I thought
    that no one would ever feel such eager love
    for those that are my kinfolk that they would keep them
    against my wishes! I knew you would not accept
    a man who is his father's killer, unholy,
    nor one whose marriage is found accursed,
    a union of mother and son.
    I knew the Areopagus, that grave council
    which belongs to this country, would not permit
    such outcasts as these to live within its realm.
    It was because I was confident of this   950
    that I laid my hands upon this quarry.
    Even then I would not have done so had he not cursed me

myself with bitter curses, and my breed.
This is what he did to me, and I determined
to give as good again. Anger knows no old age,
except in death. No sting touches the dead.
That is the case; do as you will about it.
However just my cause, I am all alone;
that makes me weak; but yet as you shall act,
old as I am, I will try to act against you.

Oedipus

Spirit lost to shame, whom does the insult light on,   960
on you or me since both of us are old?
Your mouth is wide with taunts against me—murders,
and incest and calamity, which I bore,
poor wretch, involuntarily: the gods' pleasure!
Perhaps they were angry against my people of old.
You cannot find in me, taken by myself,
an offense to reproach me with of such a greatness
to occasion such dreadful sins as I committed
against me and mine.

Tell me this:
if some god-utterance came to my father
given by oracles, that he should die by the hand   970
of his son, how can you justly taunt me with that,
who then owned neither father's seed nor mother's womb,
but was a creature still unborn?
If then I appeared, as I did to my sorrow,
and came to blows with my father and murdered him,
knowing nothing of what I did, nor who he was,
how can you be right to blame that unknowing action?
For my mother's marriage, how can you be so shameless,
villain that you are, to make me speak of this?
She was your sister. But what that marriage was
I will say now. I will not hold my tongue,   980
when you have gone so far in impious speech.

She bore me, yes, she bore me—evil on evil—
she knowing no more than I did, and having borne me
brought forth, to her shame, those children to her son.
One thing I do know: *you* know what you do,
when you speak ill of her and me for this;
but when I married her *I* did not know
nor chose; nor, as I speak of it now,
do I choose willingly to speak.
Even in this marriage I will not be reviled,
nor accept the bitter blame of father-killer
with which you have belabored me incessantly.   990
Answer me only one of my questions—this one.
If someone here and now should stand beside you
trying to kill you—such a just man as you!—
would you ask the would-be killer was he your father,
or would you pay him back for the blow at once?
I think you would, if you love your life, pay back
the man who did it; you would not look around for justice.
Into such evil I entered, for the gods
guided me to it. I do not think
that my father's spirit, alive, would gainsay that.
But you, you are no just man—you think it right   1000
to say everything, things not to be spoken,
as well as those proper to speech; you taunt me
before these people here. You speak flatteringly
of Theseus' glorious name.
You say how nobly Athens is administered.
With all your lavish praise you forget this:
that if there is a land that understands
how to worship the gods in honor, this land excels.
This is the city, I am the suppliant, old,
and you tried to steal me from it; you laid your hands
upon my daughters and made off with them.
For these your actions I call upon these Goddesses,   1010
I beseech them, I entreat them with my prayers

to come as helpers and allies; so you shall learn
indeed what sort of government guards this city.

Chorus

My lord the stranger is a good man; what has happened to him
is all in all destructive; we should help him.

Theseus

We have talked enough; those who have done this deed
are hurrying away, while we the victims stand here.

Creon

What would you have me do? I am quite helpless.

Theseus

I want you to lead the way on their tracks, and I
must go as your escort; if you have these girls 1020
still in my country, you may show them to me yourself.
If those who have them are in flight, we may spare our trouble,
for we have others to chase them. They will not escape
and fleeing from this country bless their gods for it!
Lead the way, you. Know, the taker is taken.
You were the hunter; Fortune has hunted you down.
What is gained by craft, unjustly, is not kept safely.
You need not look for anyone else to help you—
for I am sure that you were not alone
nor unprovided, seeing that you have reached
such recklessness and daring. 1030
You must have some accomplice in whom you trusted.
I must look to all of this, nor make my city
weaker than a single man. Do you understand
anything of all this? Or are my words spoken in vain
as those were that were said to you when you planned this act?

Creon

I will not fault anything you say to me
when I am here. At home they will know what to do.

Theseus

 Threaten—but go on! For you, Oedipus,
 stay here at your ease, with absolute confidence
 that if I do not die first, I will not rest   1040
 until I make your children yours again.

Oedipus

 God bless you, Theseus, for your nobleness
 and for the justice of your care for me!

Chorus

   I would I were where the wheeling charge
   of foemen soon will join
   in fight to the clash of bronze,
   on Pythian shores or the torch-lighted strand
   where the Sacred Ones cherish
   their solemn rites for mortal men,   1050
   on whose tongues the golden key rested
   of the ministrant Eumolpidae.

   There, I think, they shall reunite—
   our Theseus, rouser of battles,
   and the two captive sister maids,
   in the midst of the warring of men strong to save,
   still within Attic bounds.

   But perhaps it is where they approach
   the pastures of the west   1060
   of Oea's rock, snow-clad,
   the prisoners riding or carried in chariots,
   pushed to racing speed.

   Creon will lose. Terrible is the might
   of those that neighbor Colonus,
   and terrible the might
   of Theseus' folk.
   Every bit shines, like a lightning flash.
   Each horseman in eagerness rides,
   with loosened bridle rein.

They are the horsemen who honor   1070
Athene, goddess of horsemanship,
and the Sea Lord, Earth shaker,
dear son of Rhea.
Is the action started, or yet to come?
My mind gives me hints of hope
soon again to see the two girls
so cruelly tried,
so cruelly suffering
at the hands of their kinfolk.
Zeus will bring something to pass;
he will—and on this day.
I am the prophet
of happy outcome.
I would I were a dove in the sky,
quick of wing,
to reach a cloud over the fight   1080
with eyes lifted above the fight.

O supreme ruler of Gods,
Zeus who sees everything,
grant that those who hold this land
may achieve triumph, may win the prize
with strength victorious.

Holy daughter of Zeus,
Pallas Athene, grant it,
and you Apollo, the hunter,   1090
and your sister, the follower
of dappled deer. I beg you
for help to come doubly—
for this land and for its citizens.

Stranger and wanderer, you will not say
that I who watched on your behalf
was a false prophet. For I see
the girls returning here, and escorted, too.

Oedipus
Where? Where? What are you saying? How can it be?

Antigone
Father, O father! that some god would grant you   1100
to see this noble man who brought us home!

Oedipus
My dear, are you both here?

Antigone
Yes, for the hands
of Theseus and his dear servants rescued us.

Oedipus
Come to your father, child, and let me touch
that body I never hoped would come again!

Antigone
You shall have your wish. What you beg of us
is all our longing, too.

Oedipus
Where, oh where are you?

Antigone
Here, we are right beside you.

Oedipus
Dear children!

Antigone
All a father's love is there.

Oedipus
You loves, that have supported me!

Antigone
Poor daughters, and poor father!

Oedipus
I have what I love most. Were I still to die now,   1110
I would not be wholly wretched,

for now I have you two beside me.
Press on me, you on this side, you on that,
clinging to your father; rest yourselves now
from all the old wandering, lonely and unhappy.
And tell me, but as shortly as you can
what has happened. For girls like you
a short tale suffices.

Antigone

Here is the man who rescued us. Hear him, father.
He did it all—so shall my telling
be brief enough.

Oedipus

Sir, do not wonder that with seeming obstinacy
I prolong this conversation with my children;   1120
so utterly unexpected is what has happened!
But I know well that from none else than you
my joy in these has come to pass. You, you
it is that saved me, you and no other man.
May the gods grant all that I wish for you,
for you and for this country! Only in this people
of yours have I found piety towards the gods,
and human feeling and no hypocrisy.
I know all this—and with these words alone
do I requite what you have done. I have
all that I have through you and no one else.
My lord, reach me your right hand; let me touch it   1130
and let me kiss your head—if that is lawful.

What am I saying? How can a wretched being,
such as I have become, wish to touch *you,*
a man in whom no single stain of evil
has dwelling place? I and you cannot do so.
Nor will I suffer it to be. The possibility
of sharing in my misery is only
for those already in it.
Stand where you are. God bless you where you stand!

In the days to come may you look after me
with the justice you have shown me in this hour!

Theseus
Even if you had extended your words longer,
I would not have wondered—for your delight in your children. 1140
Nor would I, if you preferred their words to mine.
I have no weight of vexation at that.
I would have my life one of distinction,
not so much in words—rather by deeds achieved.
I let you see that what I swore to you
old man, I have not proved false to—not in anything.
For here I come, bringing your girls with me,
alive, untouched by all the threats against them.
How the fight was won, why should I boast pointlessly?
You yourself from these two will know all.

But there *is* something of question that has happened to me   1150
as I came here; let me have your counsel on it.
It is little to tell, but remarkable. No man
should treat of anything as insignificant.

Oedipus
What is it, son of Aegeus? Tell me.
I do not know what it is you ask about.

Theseus
They say there is a man, no countryman
of yours, but of your kinfolk,
who had, it would seem, thrown himself down before
the altar of Poseidon, has taken his station there. It was
where I was sacrificing, when I came here to you.

Oedipus
What countryman is he? What does he want,   1160
that he sits there as suppliant?

Theseus
                    I only know one thing.
He asks some little speech with you. This is no great matter.

Oedipus

What can it be? His suppliant seat there does not
suggest some trivial matter.

Theseus

What they say
is that he asks only to talk with you
and go away without suffering for coming here.

Oedipus

Who can he be that makes this supplication?

Theseus

Reflect if there be anyone in Argos
akin to you, that he might ask this favor.

Oedipus

Dearest of friends, stop right where you are!

Theseus

What is it?

Oedipus

Do not beg this of me.

Theseus

What is it, that I should not?   1170

Oedipus

As I hear you, I know who this suppliant is.

Theseus

And who is he that I should find fault with him?

Oedipus

He is my son, prince, he is my hated son,
whose words would hurt my ears more than all others.

Theseus

What is this? Surely it's possible
to listen and not do what you do not want?
Why should it be so bitter to you to *hear* him?

Oedipus

His voice, prince, has become a thing most hateful
to me his father; do not constrain me
to yield in this.

Theseus

Consider if it be not his suppliancy
that makes your yielding a necessity.
Perhaps regard for the god should make you careful.   1180

Antigone

Father, let me persuade you, though I am young to advise.
Suffer the king here to gratify his own heart
and give the god what the prince would have you give him.
For our sake *(pointing to her sister),* suffer our brother to come here.
He will not tear you from your resolution—
do not fear that—if he pleads what is unfit.
What harm is there in hearing what he says?
Evil contrivings are best revealed in speech.
You begot him; even if what he does to you   1190
is the most impious of all that is vile,
you ought not, father, to match him in evil.
No, let him come. Other men have had bad sons,
and have had sharp tempers.
But when they were schooled by friends' enchanting voices
their natures yield to the might of them. You,
look to that other time—not now—
the father-and-mother evils that you suffered.
If you look at that other time, I am sure,
you will know the evil end of anger, the evil
which comes to climax in it. What your heart tells you then
are not slight things—when you lost those eyes, now sightless.   1200
Yield to us all; it is not right
that those who ask what is just should have to be
importunate; nor that the man himself
who has had good treatment should not know how
to pay requital for it.

Oedipus

My child, when you win me with your words,
it is a bitter pleasure to yield. Let it be so,
as you will have it. Only, sir, if he comes here
let no one have the disposal of my life.

Theseus

Once is enough for that. I do not need to hear it twice,
old man; I do not want to boast, but you,
you know you are safe—if a god keeps *me* safe.   1210

Chorus

Whoever it is that seeks to have
a greater share of life,
letting moderation slip out of his thoughts,
I count him a fool, a persistent fool;
I am clear in my mind of that.

Indeed, the long days store up many things
that are nearer to sorrow than joy,
and the whereabouts of delight
you will not find, once you have fallen
into the region beyond your due term.
The Helper still is the same for all,
the same Consummator,   1220
Death at the last,
the appearance of Death in Doom.
He comes to no sound of wedding joy,
no lyre, no dances.

Not to be born is best of all;
when life is there, the second best
to go hence where you came,
with the best speed you may.
For when his youth with its gift of light heart   1230
has come and gone, what grievous stroke
is spared to a man, what agony
is he without? Envy, and faction,

strife and fighting and murders are his,
and yet there is something more that claims him,
old age at the last, most hated,
without power, without comrades, and friends,
when every ill, all ills,
take up their dwelling with him.
So, he is old—this old man here—
I am not alone in that,
as the wave-lashed cape that faces north,   1240
in the wintertime,
the din of the winds on every side,
the din of the mischiefs encompass him utterly,
like the breaking crests of the waves forever,
some from the setting sun,
some from his rising,
and some from the place of his midday beams,
and some from the northern mountains of night.

Antigone
   Here he is, it seems, this stranger,
   alone, my father, weeping his tears in floods,   1250
   as he comes here.

Oedipus
   Who is it?

Antigone
         He whom we always held in mind
   that it would be; here is Polyneices.

Polyneices
   O, what shall I do?
   Shall I cry for my own troubles, first of all,
   my sisters? Or his, my old father's,
   as I see them before me?
   Here I find him in a foreign country,
   an exile banished here, with clothes upon him
   where the foul ancient dirt has lived so long

that it infects his old body,
and his uncombed hair floats in the wind   1260
about his eyeless face.
The food he carries to fill his belly,
is, I should guess, akin to what he wears.
I learn all this too late, wretch that I am!
I will bear witness against myself, as the world's villain,
for not supporting him. You need not learn
from others what I am.
But yet there is Mercy; in everything
she shares the throne of Zeus. Let her stand by you   1270
too, father. Why are you silent?
Say something!
Do not turn away from me giving no answer,
sending me hence dishonored by your silence,
not even telling me why you are angry.
You children of this father, blood of my blood,
will you try at least to make him open his mouth
that now denies approach, in implacable silence?
So may he not dismiss me in dishonor—
a god's suppliant that I am—with never a word.

Antigone
Speak yourself, unhappy man, say what you come to seek.   1280
The flood of words may give some kind of pleasure:
They may make angry or just bring some pity;
still, somehow, they give a voice to what is voiceless.

Polyneices
Then I will speak; your advice is good.
First, here I make the god my helper
from whose altar the prince of this country raised me up
to come to you. He granted me permission
to speak, and hear, and a safe-conduct home.
These things I would have from you, my foreign friends,
and from my sisters and my father.   1290

Father, I want to tell you why I came here.
I have been banished from my country, made an exile,
because I claimed my right as the elder born
to sit upon your sovereign throne. For this,
my younger brother, Eteocles, drove me out.
He did not have the best of me in words,
nor in the proof of hand or deed. It was the city
which he persuaded. The chief reason, I think,
was the curse, *your* curse, that lay upon the house.
That is what I hear also from the soothsayers.

When I came to the Dorian land of Argos   1300
Adrastus gave me his daughter to wife.
Then I swore to my side all
that were reputed best and honored most
for skill in warfare in the Apian land,
that I might gather from these a seven-fold band
of spearmen against Thebes; then with justice on my side
either die—or banish those that had done me wrong.
Very well, then; why have I come to you?
To bring, my father, my suppliant prayers, for myself
and for my allies, who with seven hosts   1310
behind their seven spears encompass about
the entire plain of Thebes.

There is the spearman, Amphiareus, supreme
master in war, supreme in knowledge of omens;
the second is the Aetolian, son of Oeneus,
Tydeus; third Eteoclus, born an Argive;
the fourth Hippomedon, sent by his father Talaos;
the fifth Capaneus, who has vowed to burn
the city of Thebes into the ground; the sixth   1320
Parthenopaeus, the Arcadian, hastens to the war,
his name recalling his mother, long a virgin
but brought at last to travail by the trusty
son of Atalanta;
and then myself, yours but not yours, begotten

of an evil fate, yet called at least your son,
I lead the fearless host of Argos to Thebes.

We all entreat you, by these your children, by
your life, my father, remit your heavy anger
against me, as I set forth to punish my brother
who thrust me out, despoiled me of my country.   1330
For if there is any trust to be placed in oracles,
they have said the victory shall come to those
whose side you join.
Then, by our fountains, and our race's gods,
I beg you to be persuaded and to yield.
We are beggars and foreigners both—and so are you!
We live by flattering others, both you and I.
We have drawn the selfsame lot in life.
But he is a prince, at home—oh wretched me!—
and laughs at both of us, in luxury.
If you will stand a helper to my purpose   1340
I will shake him out of it with little trouble
and quick enough, so that I can place you again
in your own house and place myself there too,
once I have driven him out and forcefully.
I may make this my boast if you stand by me,
without you I have no strength, even to survive.

Chorus
Oedipus, as to this man,
out of consideration for him that sent him here,
say what is proper and send him on his way.

Oedipus
Yes, public guardians of this land, I will.
If he that sent him to me had not been
Theseus, who thought it right that he should hear   1350
words of mine, he never would have heard my voice.
But now he will go hence, having been thought worthy
and heard from me such words as never will
gladden his life.

You scoundrel, you, with your scepter and your throne—
held now by your blood brother in Thebes—
you chased me out, your father, made me cityless;
these are the clothes *you* made me wear,
the sight of which now brings tears to your eyes,
when *you* have come to the same stress of misery.
I may not weep, *I* must put up with it   1360
as long as I live remembering my murderer;
you have contrived my rearing in agony;
you drove me out. It is because of you
I am a wanderer begging my daily bread.
Had I not begotten these children to be my nurses
I had been dead, for all you did to help.
Now it is they who save me, these very nurses.
They are men, not women, in bearing troubles with me.
You are no sons of mine, you are someone else's.
Therefore the Evil Spirit has eyes upon you,   1370
although, by and by, those eyes will be still fiercer,
if these hosts are really moving towards Thebes.
That city you will not destroy—no, before that
you will fall yourself, polluted with blood, and equally
your brother. Such are the curses I sent forth
in days gone by, against you two. And now
I summon those curses to come to me as allies,
that you two, brothers, may know to reverence parents,
and not dishonor a father because he was blind—
and got such men as you for sons. These girls
have done none of this.
Therefore my curses overcome   1380
your suppliant seat, and that, your throne, in Thebes,
as sure as Justice, claimed of old time, is sharer
in Zeus' throne, by the might of the old laws.
Get you gone! I spit you from me. I am no father
of yours, you worst of villains! Pack away
all of these curses that I invoke against you.
You shall not conquer by spear your native land;

you shall not come again to hollow Argos;
you are to die by a brother's hand, and kill him
by whom you were exiled.
There are my curses on you! And I summon
your father's hateful darkness of Tartarus   1390
to give you a new dwelling place. I call
upon the spirits there, I call on Ares,
that thrust upon you both this dreadful hatred.

That is what you have heard. Now, off with you and tell
all the Cadmeans and your trusty allies
that such are the honors Oedipus divided
between those sons of his!

Chorus
    I had no pleasure, Polyneices,
    in your past journeyings. Now, speedily back again!

Polyneices
    Woe for my journey! woe for its ill success!
    Woe for my comrades! what an end this road had   1400
    when we set out from Argos! woe is me!
    such an end that I cannot tell to any
    of those comrades, nor yet turn *them* home again!
    but, saying nothing, go on to meet my fortune.
    Sisters—for you *are* my sisters, although his daughters—
    since you have heard my father's dreadful curses,
    I pray you two, by the gods, if the day come
    when his curses come to pass, and you have somehow
    come home again, do not dishonor me,
    but lay me in a grave with funeral rites.   1410
    You have praise now, for the pains that you took,
    in caring for this old man; you will earn no less
    besides for helping me.

Antigone
    Polyneices, I entreat you,
    do the thing that I ask you.

Polyneices
  Dearest Antigone,
  what is it? Tell me.

Antigone
  Turn your army
  back to Argos speedily. Do not
  destroy yourself and the city both.

Polyneices
  I cannot
  do this. How can I lead this selfsame army
  back again when I have once
  proved myself coward?

Antigone
  Why must you, brother, fall to anger again?   1420
  If you destroy your own country, what do you gain?

Polyneices
  Exile is shameful, and shameful that one elder
  be so mocked by his brother.

Antigone
  Do you see, then,
  how right our father's prophecies come out
  when he spoke of the mutual murder of you two?

Polyneices
  That is what *he* wants. But I must not yield.

Antigone
  Wretched that I am! But who, once he has heard
  our father's prophecies, will dare to follow you?

Polyneices
  I will not tell bad news. That is good generalship—
  to tell one's strengths and not one's weaknesses.   1430

Antigone
  Then, brother, you are truly so determined?

Polyneices

Do not stop me. Now this must be my care,
this road of mine, ill-omened and terrible,
made so by my father and those Furies of his;
but may Zeus prosper *your* road, if you fulfill
my wishes, at my death. For me in life
there is nothing you can do. Let me go now,
and, both of you, goodbye. You will never again
see me alive.

Antigone

My heart is broken!

Polyneices

Do not mourn for me.

Antigone

Brother, how can anyone
not mourn, seeing you set out
to death so clear before you?

1440

Polyneices

If die I must, I'll die.

Antigone

Do not, dearest;
do as I say.

Polyneices

Do not try to persuade me
to fail my duty.

Antigone

Then I am utterly
destroyed if I must lose you.

Polyneices

All of that
whether for good or ill, Fortune determines.
But for you two, I pray the gods that never

you meet with ill. In all men's judgment
you should not suffer misfortune.

Chorus

> Here are other new ills that have come
> just now, of evil doom,
> from the blind stranger—
> unless Fate is somehow at work.   1450
> For I cannot call any decision of God
> a vain thing.
> Time watches constantly those decisions;
> Some fortunes it destroys, and others,
> on the day following, lifts up again.

> There is the thunder! Zeus!

Oedipus

My children, children, please can someone go
and fetch for me Theseus that best of men?

Antigone

Father, what is the occasion of your summons?

Oedipus

The winged thunder of Zeus will carry me   1460
straightway to death. Send and send quickly!

Chorus

Look at it! rolling down, crashing,
the thunderbolt unspeakable, hurled by Zeus.
Terror has raised the hair on my head;
my heart is trembling.
There, again, is the flash of the lightning!
It burns in the sky. What event will it yield?
I am all fear. It is not for nothing
when it lightens so; there will be issue of it.   1470
O, the great sky! O Zeus!

Oedipus

Children, there has come to me, as the gods said,
my end of life. There is no more turning away.

Antigone

    How do you know? What makes you think it?

Oedipus

    I know it well. But, quickly, someone go
    and summon here this country's prince.

Chorus

    See, there again, around us
    the piercing thunder!
    Be merciful, God, if you are bringing   1480
    some black-night thing
    to this land, our mother.
    May I find you gracious.
    Because I have looked on a man accursed
    may I not have a share in a graceless grace!
    Lord Zeus, to you I cry.

Oedipus

    Is the man near? And children, will he find me
    still alive and my wits not astray?

Antigone

    What confidence would you implant in his mind?

Oedipus

    That, for the kindness he has shown me, the requital,
    as I once promised, now is duly paid.   1490

Chorus

    My son, come here,
    or if in the innermost recess of the glade
    you are hallowing Poseidon's altar
    with sacrifice of cattle, come still.
    For the stranger claims to make return
    to you, and the city and his friends,
    a just return for a just kindness done.

Theseus

    What is this public summons from all of you,   1500
    clearly from my people, clearly from this stranger?

Is it the thunder of Zeus or rushing hail?
One can indeed conjecture anything
when Zeus sends such a storm.

Oedipus

My lord, I have longed for you and you have come.
Some god has made for you a happy blessing
from this coming.

Theseus

What new thing is it, son of Laius?

Oedipus

The balance of my life's scale has come down.
I will not choose to fail my promises
to you and the city, now, before I die.

Theseus

What evidence have you of this impending death?   1510

Oedipus

The gods are their own messengers to me;
they are not false to the signs they have arranged.

Theseus

What signs? Make this clear, old man.

Oedipus

The long continued thunder, the massive lightning
hurled from the hand that never knew defeat.

Theseus

I believe you; for I have seen you prophesy
much, and falsely never. Tell me what to do.

Oedipus

Yes; I will direct you, son of Aegeus,
in what shall be a treasure for this city.
Old age shall not decay it. Immediately
I will show the way without a hand to guide me   1520
to the place where I must die.
And you, describe this to no man, ever,

neither where it is hidden nor in what region,
that doing so may make you a defense
beyond the worth of many shields, or many neighbors' help.
The things within this ban, not to be uttered,
yourself shall learn, when you come there alone,
for I shall not declare them to anyone
of these citizens, nor to my daughters, dear though I hold them.
Keep them yourself always, and when you come   1530
to the end of life reveal them only
to him that is nearest to you, and he in turn
to his successor.
So you shall hold this city undevastated
by the Sown Men. Ten thousand states
have committed violence on one another,
despite their rulers' excellent government.
For the gods are careful watchers at the last
but slow in action, when one dismissing gods' will
has turned to madness. Never
let that befall you, son of Aegeus.
But I will not school you in such things; you know them.
Let us now go to the place—a pressing summons   1540
from the god forces me—and delay no more.
My children, follow me—so. In a strange way
I have become your guide; you were once mine.
Come on, but touch me not. Suffer me to find
my sacred grave where it is fated
that I shall be hidden in this country's earth.
This way, this way, like this! For this way Hermes,
the Conductor, leads me, and the goddess of the dead.
O light, no light though you were once a light
to me! now for the last time touch my body.   1550
For I creep along to hide my last of life
in Hades. You dearest of friends (to Theseus)
yourself, this land and these your citizens—
blessings upon you! and in your blessedness
remember me, the dead! Live blessed forever.

Chorus

    If it be lawful, it is mine
    to adore with prayers the Goddess Unseen
    and you, my lord of the Creatures of Night,
    Aidoneus, Aidoneus,
    that our stranger friend may pass to his end   1560
    untroubled and free of the tears
    attendant on a grievous doom;
    that he may come to the world below,
    that hides all within itself,
    to the land of the dead, the Stygian house.
    Many the ills that were his, all uncalled for;
    may God in justice exalt him again!

    O goddesses of that Underworld,
    and Form of the Hound Unconquered
    who keeps his lair at the guest-haunted gate,   1570
    and sleeps and snuffles from out his cave,
    the guardian in death's house, unsubdued—
    thus is always the story told.

    O son of Earth and Tartarus
    I pray that that Hound may give a clear path
    to our friend coming down
    to dead men's country;
    You, Giver of Sleep Everlasting,
    I call on You.

Messenger

    Citizens: to speak most briefly and truthfully,
    Oedipus is gone. But what has happened,   1580
    the tale of that cannot be told so briefly,
    for the acts there were not brief.

Chorus

    The unhappy man is gone!

Messenger

    You must think of him
    as of one truly parted out of life.

Chorus

    How was it? By God's chance and painlessly
    the poor man ended?

Messenger

    That is wonderful indeed.
    How he moved from here with no guidance of friends,
    you yourselves know. For I think you were here.
    He was himself the guide to all of us.
    When he came to the steep road, rooted in earth   1590
    by brazen steps, he stood in one of the many
    branching paths, near the hollow basin
    where is, forever confident, the memorial
    to Theseus' and Peirithous' compact.
    Where he stood, he was midway between
    that basin and the Thorician rock,
    the hollow pear tree and the grave of stone.

    Then he sat down and loosed his filthy robes,
    cried loudly to his daughters to bring him water
    from some stream, to wash and make drink offerings.
    They hurried to Demeter's hill, in front of them,   1600
    guardian of tender plants; they brought what he ordered;
    and then with lustral washing and with clothes
    equipped him in the customary fashion.
    When he had his pleasure of all he did,
    and nothing that he sought was scanted, Zeus
    of the Underworld thundered. They fell at their father's knees
    and cried, ceaselessly, beating their breasts,
    and with unending long laments. But he,
    when he heard the sudden bitter cries from them,   1610
    folded his hands upon them; then said "My children,
    this is the day when you become fatherless.
    All that was me has perished; now no more

for you the heavy task of tending me.
It was a cruel task, children, that I know,
but there's a single word that overthrows
all tasks of work. My love you had; no one
could love you more. That is the love you lose now
and must pass through the rest of life without it."
They embraced and sobbed shrilly, all three of them.   1620
When they came to the end of their mourning
and not another cry rose, there, in the stillness,
there was a voice of someone, summoning him,
and suddenly in their terror, all hair stood up.
It was the god who called him, over and over,
"You, Oedipus, Oedipus, why are you hesitating
to go our way? You have been too slow, too long."
When he understood that calling of the god,
he cried to this country's ruler, Theseus,   1630
to come to him, and when he came, he said:
"You that I love, give me your hand's sworn pledge
to these my children, and you, my children, to him.
Promise me that you will never consciously
forsake them, but perform whatever you judge
will be for their advantage always."
He, noble man that he is, gave him his promise
and with no word of sorrow swore he would do
that, for his friend.
When he had finished, suddenly Oedipus
touching his children with blind hands said, "Both, my children,   1640
be brave and noble of mind, and leave this place.
Do not seek to know what is forbidden,
nor hear it from others' speaking.
Quickly, away with you; only let Theseus
stay to understand what is to be done."

That was what he said; we listened all,
and with the girls in tears and lamentations,
followed them away. When we departed,

in a few moments we looked back and saw that
Oedipus, yes, Oedipus, was no longer there,
but the king by himself, holding his hand
before his face, to shade his eyes, as though   1650
some deadly terror had appeared to him
that sight could not endure.
Then just a little afterwards, we saw him
bow to salute the earth and the gods' Olympus
united in the same prayer at once.
But by what manner of doom that other died
no mortal man can say, save our lord Theseus.
It was no fiery thunderbolt of God
that made away with him, nor a sea hurricane   1660
rising; no, it was some messenger
sent by the gods, or some power of the dead
split open the fundament of earth, with good will,
to give him painless entry. He was sent on his way
with no accompaniment of tears, no pain of sickness;
if any man ended miraculously,
this man did. If I seem to talk nonsense,
I would not try to win over such as think so.

Chorus
    Where are the girls? And where their escorting friends?

Messenger
    Not far away. The sounds of their mourning voices
    show they are coming here.

Antigone
    Now it belongs to both of us,   1670
    unhappy beings, to sorrow
    for the curse that inheres
    in our father's blood;
    not for this part, yes, and for that part, no—
    totally.
    For him we have borne in his life
    a great burden unrelieved,

but now at the end we will have to speak
of things beyond reason's scope,
what we saw, what we suffered.

Chorus

What is it?

Antigone

My friends, we can only guess.

Chorus

He has gone?

Antigone

As you would have him go.
What else can be said of one
whom neither the War God,
nor the sea encountered,   1680
but the unseen fields of the world of Death
snatched away in some doom invisible?
On us two destruction's night
has settled on our eyes.
How shall we wander, how find
a bitter living in distant lands
or on the waves of the sea?

Ismene

I do not know.
Let murdering Hades
take me and join me in death with him,   1690
my father in his old age.
The life that will henceforth be mine
is a life that cannot be lived.

Chorus

You two are the best of children;
you must bear what the god gives to bear.
No more fire of grief. You cannot truly
sorrow for what has happened.

Antigone
> There can be a love
> even of suffering;
> for that which is anything but dear itself
> could still be dear,
> while I still had him in these hands of mine.
> Father, dear one, you that forever   1700
> have put on the darkness of underground,
> even there you shall not be unloved,
> by me and by my sister.

Chorus
> His end?

Antigone
> His end is what he wished.

Chorus
> What end?

Antigone
> And he died in a foreign land,
> but one he yearned for. He has his bed
> below in the shadowy grass
> forever.
> He has left behind him a mourning sorrow—
> these eyes of mine with their tears
> bewail you. I do not know how   1710
> in my misery I should cast out
> such a weight of sorrow.
> Yes, you chose in a foreign land
> to die. I find it a lonely death.

Ismene
> What further destiny awaits
> you and me, dear one, alone as we are?

Chorus
　My dears, the end of his life was blessed;　　　　　　1720
　do not keep sorrowing. No one
　is hard for misfortune to capture.

Antigone
　Let us hurry back, sister.

Ismene
　What to do?

Antigone
　Desire possesses me—

Ismene
　What desire?

Antigone
　To see where he lies in earth.

Ismene
　Who lies?

Antigone
　Our father—Oh, misery!

Ismene
　How can that be lawful?
　Do you not see?

Antigone
　Why do you blame me for this?　　　　　　　　　　1730

Ismene
　And this again—

Antigone
　What is *this* again?

Ismene
　Where he fell, there *is* no grave—
　and he was quite alone.

Antigone
> Bring me where he was,
> and then kill me.

Ismene
> Where now so lonely,
> so helpless, shall *I* live?

Chorus
> Friends, do not be afraid!

Antigone
> But where to find refuge?

Chorus
> You *have* found refuge.

Antigone
> From what?

Chorus
> From misfortune, refuge for you both.   1740

Antigone
> I understand.

Chorus
> What is it you are thinking?

Antigone
> I cannot tell
> how I can come home.

Chorus
> Do not seek to go home.

Antigone
> Trouble is upon us.

Chorus
> It has pursued you before.

Antigone
> Desperate then, but now still worse.

Chorus
    Yes, yours was a sea of sorrow.

Antigone
    Where shall we go, O God?
    To what of hope now
    can Fate drive us?   1750

(Theseus enters.)

Theseus
    Cease your mourning, children; for those
    to whom the grace of the Underworld Gods
    has been stored as a treasure, to the quick and the dead,
    for them there shall be no mourning.
    Else the gods may be angry.

Antigone
    Son of Aegeus, we beg you—

Theseus
    What would you have me grant, children?

Antigone
    We would ourselves see the grave
    of our father.

Theseus
    No, this is not lawful.

Antigone
    What do you mean, king of Athens?

Theseus
    He   1760
    has forbidden approach to the place,
    nor may any voice invoke
    the sacred tomb where he lies.
    He said, if I truly did this,
    I should have forever a land unharmed.

These pledges the God heard from me
and Oath, Zeus' servant, all seeing.

Antigone

If this was, then, the mind of Him,
the dead, I must be content.
Send us, then, to our ancient Thebes   1770
that perhaps we may prevent
the murder that comes to our brothers.

Theseus

That I will do and whatever else
shall profit yourselves and pleasure both you
and the man under earth who is newly gone—
for him I must spare no pains.

Chorus

Now cease lamentation, nor further prolong
your dirge. All of these matters
have found their consummation.

ANTIGONE

Translated by David Grene

CHARACTERS

Antigone

Ismene

Chorus of Theban Elders

Creon

A Sentry

Haemon

Teiresias

A Messenger

Eurydice

Second Messenger

ANTIGONE

(The two sisters Antigone and Ismene meet in front of the palace gates in Thebes.)

Antigone

    Ismene, my dear sister,
    whose father was my father, can you think of any
    of all the evils that stem from Oedipus
    that Zeus does not bring to pass for us, while we yet live?
    No pain, no ruin, no shame, and no dishonor   5
    but I have seen it in our mischiefs,
    yours and mine.
    And now what is the proclamation that they tell of
    made lately by the commander, publicly,
    to all the people? Do you know it? Have you heard it?
    Don't you notice when the evils due to enemies
    are headed towards those we love?   10

Ismene

    Not a word, Antigone, of those we love,
    either sweet or bitter, has come to me since the moment
    when we lost our two brothers,
    on one day, by their hands dealing mutual death.
    Since the Argive army fled in this past night,   15
    I know of nothing further, nothing
    of better fortune or of more destruction.

Antigone

    I knew it well; that is why I sent for you
    to come outside the palace gates
    to listen to me, privately.

Ismene

    What is it? Certainly your words   20
    come of dark thoughts.

Antigone

    Yes, indeed; for those two brothers of ours, in burial
    has not Creon honored the one, dishonored the other?
    Eteocles, they say he has used justly
    with lawful rites and hid him in the earth
    to have his honor among the dead men there.
    But the unhappy corpse of Polyneices
    he has proclaimed to all the citizens,
    they say, no man may hide
    in a grave nor mourn in funeral,
    but leave unwept, unburied, a dainty treasure
    for the birds that see him, for their feast's delight.   30
    That is what, they say, the worthy Creon
    has proclaimed for you and me—for me, I tell you—
    and he comes here to clarify to the unknowing
    his proclamation; he takes it seriously;
    for whoever breaks the edict death is prescribed,
    and death by stoning publicly.
    There you have it; soon you will show yourself
    as noble both in your nature and your birth,
    or yourself as base, although of noble parents.

Ismene

    If things are as you say, poor sister, how
    can I better them? how loose or tie the knot?   40

Antigone

    Decide if you will share the work, the deed.

Ismene

    What kind of danger is there? How far have your thoughts gone?

Antigone

    Here is this hand. Will you help it to lift the dead man?

Ismene

    Would you bury him, when it is forbidden the city?

Antigone

    At least he is my brother—and yours, too,
    though you deny him. *I* will not prove false to him.

Ismene
    You are so headstrong. Creon has forbidden it.

Antigone
    It is not for him to keep me from my own.

Ismene
    O God!
    Consider, sister, how our father died,
    hated and infamous; how he brought to light   50
    his own offenses; how he himself struck out
    the sight of his two eyes;
    his own hand was their executioner.
    Then, mother and wife, two names in one, did shame
    violently on her life, with twisted cords.
    Third, our two brothers, on a single day,
    poor wretches, themselves worked out their mutual doom.
    Each killed the other, hand against brother's hand.
    Now there are only the two of us, left behind,
    and see how miserable our end shall be
    if in the teeth of law we shall transgress
    against the sovereign's decree and power.   60
    You ought to realize we are only women,
    not meant in nature to fight against men,
    and that we are ruled, by those who are stronger,
    to obedience in this and even more painful matters.
    I do indeed beg those beneath the earth
    to give me their forgiveness,
    since force constrains me,
    that I shall yield in this to the authorities.
    Extravagant action is not sensible.

Antigone
    I would not urge you now; nor if you wanted
    to act would I be glad to have you with me.   70
    Be as you choose to be; but for myself
    I myself will bury him. It will be good
    to die, so doing. I shall lie by his side,

loving him as he loved me; I shall be
a criminal—but a religious one.
The time in which I must please those that are dead
is longer than I must please those of this world.
For there I shall lie forever. You, if you like,
can cast dishonor on what the gods have honored.

Ismene

I will not put dishonor on them, but
to act in defiance of the citizenry,
my nature does not give me means for that.

Antigone

Let that be your excuse. But I will go   80
to heap the earth on the grave of my loved brother.

Ismene

How I fear for you, my poor sister!

Antigone

Do not fear for me. Make straight your own path to destiny.

Ismene

At least do not speak of this act to anyone else;
bury him in secret; I will be silent, too.

Antigone

Oh, oh, no! shout it out. I will hate you still worse
for silence—should you not proclaim it,
to everyone.

Ismene

You have a warm heart for such chilly deeds.

Antigone

I know I am pleasing those I should please most.

Ismene

If you can do it. But you are in love   90
with the impossible.

Antigone

No. When I can no more, then I will stop.

Ismene

It is better not to hunt the impossible
at all.

Antigone

If you will talk like this I will loathe you,
and you will be adjudged an enemy—
justly—by the dead's decision. Let me alone
and my folly with me, to endure this terror.
No suffering of mine will be enough
to make me die ignobly.

Ismene

Well, if you will, go on.
Know this; that though you are wrong to go, your friends
are right to love you.

Chorus

    Sun's beam, fairest of all   100
    that ever till now shone
    on seven-gated Thebes;
    O golden eye of day, you shone
    coming over Dirce's stream;
    You drove in headlong rout
    the whiteshielded man from Argos,
    complete in arms;
    his bits rang sharper
    under your urging.

    Polyneices brought him here   110
    against our land, Polyneices,
    roused by contentious quarrel;
    like an eagle he flew into our country,
    with many men-at-arms,
    with many a helmet crowned with horsehair.

He stood above the halls, gaping with murderous lances,
encompassing the city's
seven-gated mouth.
But before his jaws would be sated
with our blood, before the fire,   120
pine fed, should capture our crown of towers,
he went hence—
such clamor of war stretched behind his back,
from his dragon foe, a thing he could not overcome.

For Zeus, who hates the most
the boasts of a great tongue,
saw them coming in a great tide,
insolent in the clang of golden armor.   130
The god struck him down with hurled fire,
as he strove to raise the victory cry,
now at the very winning post.

The earth rose to strike him as he fell swinging.
In his frantic onslaught, possessed, he breathed upon us
with blasting winds of hate.
Sometimes the great god of war was on one side,
and sometimes he struck a staggering blow on the other;
the god was a very wheel horse on the right trace.   140

At seven gates stood seven captains,
ranged equals against equals, and there left
their brazen suits of armor
to Zeus, the god of trophies.
Only those two wretches born of one father and mother
set their spears to win a victory on both sides;
they worked out their share in a common death.

Now Victory, whose name is great, has come
to Thebes of many chariots
with joy to answer her joy,
to bring forgetfulness of these wars;   150
let us go to all the shrines of the gods

and dance all night long.
Let Bacchus lead the dance,
shaking Thebes to trembling.

But here is the king of our land,
Creon, son of Menoeceus;
in our new contingencies with the gods,
he is our new ruler.
He comes to set in motion some design—
what design is it? Because he has proposed   160
the convocation of the elders.
He sent a public summons for our discussion.

Creon

Gentlemen: as for our city's fortune,
the gods have shaken her, when the great waves broke,
but the gods have brought her through again to safety.
For yourselves, I chose you out of all and summoned you
to come to me, partly because I knew you
as always loyal to the throne—at first,
when Laïus was king, and then again
when Oedipus saved our city and then again
when he died and you remained with steadfast truth
to their descendants,
until they met their double fate upon one day,
striking and stricken, defiled each by a brother's murder.   170
Now here I am, holding all authority
and the throne, in virtue of kinship with the dead.

It is impossible to know any man—
I mean his soul, intelligence, and judgment—
until he shows his skill in rule and law.
I think that a man supreme ruler of a whole city,
if he does not reach for the best counsel for her,
but through some fear, keeps his tongue under lock and key,   180
him I judge the worst of any;
I have always judged so; and anyone thinking
another man more a friend than his own country,

I rate him nowhere. For my part, God is my witness,
who sees all, always, I would not be silent
if I saw ruin, not safety, on the way
towards my fellow citizens. I would not count
any enemy of my country as a friend—
because of what I know, that she it is
which gives us our security. If she sails upright
and we sail on her, friends will be ours for the making.   190
In the light of rules like these, I will make her greater still.

In consonance with this, I here proclaim
to the citizens about Oedipus' sons.
For Eteocles, who died this city's champion,
showing his valor's supremacy everywhere,
he shall be buried in his grave with every rite
of sanctity given to heroes under earth.
However, his brother, Polyneices, a returned exile,
who sought to burn with fire from top to bottom
his native city, and the gods of his own people;   200
who sought to taste the blood he shared with us,
and lead the rest of us to slavery—
I here proclaim to the city that this man
shall no one honor with a grave and none shall mourn.
You shall leave him without burial; you shall watch him
chewed up by birds and dogs and violated.
Such is my mind in the matter; never by me
shall the wicked man have precedence in honor
over the just. But he that is loyal to the state
in death, in life alike, shall have my honor.   210

Chorus

Son of Menoeceus, so it is your pleasure
to deal with foe and friend of this our city.
To use any legal means lies in your power,
both about the dead and those of us who live.

Creon

I understand, then, you will do my bidding.

Chorus
  Please lay this burden on some younger man.

Creon
  Oh, watchers of the corpse I have already.

Chorus
  What else, then, do your commands entail?

Creon
  That you should not side with those who disagree.

Chorus
  There is none so foolish as to love his own death.   220

Creon
  Yes, indeed those are the wages, but often greed
  has with its hopes brought men to ruin.

[*The sentry whose speeches follow represents a remarkable experi-
ment in Greek tragedy in the direction of naturalism of speech. He
speaks with marked clumsiness, partly because he is excited and talks
almost colloquially. But also the royal presence makes him think apparently that he should be rather grand in his show of respect. He uses odd
bits of archaism or somewhat stale poetical passages, particularly in catch
phrases. He sounds something like lower-level Shakespearean characters, e.g. Constable Elbow, with his uncertainty about benefactor and
malefactor.*]

Sentry
  My lord, I will never claim my shortness of breath
  is due to hurrying, nor were there wings in my feet.
  I stopped at many a lay-by in my thinking;
  I circled myself till I met myself coming back.
  My soul accosted me with different speeches.
  "Poor fool, yourself, why are you going somewhere
  when once you get there you will pay the piper?"
  "Well, aren't you the daring fellow! stopping again?
  and suppose Creon hears the news from someone else—

don't you realize that you will smart for that?"   230
I turned the whole matter over. I suppose I may say
"I made haste slowly" and the short road became long.
However, at last I came to a resolve:
I must go to you; even if what I say
is nothing, really, still I shall say it.
I come here, a man with a firm clutch on the hope
that nothing can betide him save what is fated.

Creon

What is it then that makes you so afraid?

Sentry

No, I want first of all to tell you my side of it.
I didn't do the thing; I never saw who did it.
It would not be fair for me to get into trouble.   240

Creon

You hedge, and barricade the thing itself.
Clearly you have some ugly news for me.

Sentry

Well, you know how disasters make a man
hesitate to be their messenger.

Creon

For God's sake, tell me and get out of here!

Sentry

Yes, I *will* tell you. Someone just now
buried the corpse and vanished. He scattered on the skin
some thirsty dust; he did the ritual,
duly, to purge the body of desecration.

Creon

What! Now who on earth could have done that?

Sentry

I do not know. For there was there no mark
of axe's stroke nor casting up of earth
of any mattock; the ground was hard and dry,   250

unbroken; there were no signs of wagon wheels.
The doer of the deed had left no trace.
But when the first sentry of the day pointed it out,
there was for all of us a disagreeable
wonder. For the body had disappeared;
not in a grave, of course; but there lay upon him
a little dust as of a hand avoiding
the curse of violating the dead body's sanctity.
There were no signs of any beast nor dog
that came there; he had clearly not been torn.
There was a tide of bad words at one another,
guard taunting guard, and it might well have ended   260
in blows, for there was no one there to stop it.
Each one of us was the criminal but no one
manifestly so; all denied knowledge of it.
We were ready to take hot bars in our hands
or walk through fire, and call on the gods with oaths
that we had neither done it nor were privy
to a plot with anyone, neither in planning
nor yet in execution.
At last when nothing came of all our searching,
there was one man who spoke, made every head
bow to the ground in fear. For we could not
either contradict him nor yet could we see how   270
if we did what he said we would come out all right.
His word was that we must lay information
about this matter to yourself; we could not cover it.
This view prevailed and the lot of the draw chose me,
unlucky me, to win that prize. So here
I am. I did not want to come,
and you don't want to have me. I know that.
For no one likes the messenger of bad news.

Chorus

    My lord: I wonder, could this be God's doing?
    This is the thought that keeps on haunting me.

Creon

Stop, before your words fill even me with rage,   280
that you should be exposed as a fool, and you so old.
For what you say is surely insupportable
when you say the gods took forethought for this corpse.
Is it out of excess of honor for the man,
for the favors that he did them, they should cover him?
This man who came to burn their pillared temples,
their dedicated offerings—and this land
and laws he would have scattered to the winds?
Or do you see the gods as honoring
criminals? This is not so. But what I am doing
now, and other things before this, some men disliked,   290
within this very city, and muttered against me,
secretly shaking their heads; they would not bow
justly beneath the yoke to submit to me.
I am very sure that these men hired others
to do this thing. I tell you the worse currency
that ever grew among mankind is money. This
sacks cities, this drives people from their homes,
this teaches and corrupts the minds of the loyal
to acts of shame. This displays   300
all kinds of evil for the use of men,
instructs in the knowledge of every impious act.
Those that have done this deed have been paid to do it,
but in the end they will pay for what they have done.

It is as sure as I still reverence Zeus—
know this right well—and I speak under oath—
if you and your fellows do not find this man
who with his own hand did the burial
and bring him here before me face to face,
your death alone will not be enough for me.
You will hang alive till you open up this outrage.
That will teach you in the days to come from what   310
you may draw profit—safely—from your plundering.

It's not from anything and everything
you can grow rich. You will find out
that ill-gotten gains ruin more than they save.

Sentry

Have I your leave to say something—or should I
just turn and go?

Creon

Don't you know your talk is painful enough already?

Sentry

Is the ache in your ears or in your mind?

Creon

Why do you dissect the whereabouts of my pain?

Sentry

Because it is he who did the deed who hurts
your mind. I only hurt your ears that listen.

Creon

I am sure you have been a chatterbox since you were born.   320

Sentry

All the same, I did not do this thing.

Creon

You might have done this, too, if you sold your soul.

Sentry

It's a bad thing if one judges and judges wrongly.

Creon

You may talk as wittily as you like of judgment.
Only, if you don't bring to light those men
who have done this, you will yet come to say
that your wretched gains have brought bad consequences.

Sentry (aside)

It were best that he were found, but whether
the criminal is taken or he isn't—
for that chance will decide—one thing is certain,

you'll never see me coming here again.
I never hoped to escape, never thought I could.   330
But now I have come off safe, I thank God heartily.

Chorus

Many are the wonders, none
is more wonderful than what is man.
This it is that crosses the sea
with the south winds storming and the waves swelling,
breaking around him in roaring surf.
He it is again who wears away
the Earth, oldest of gods, immortal, unwearied,
as the ploughs wind across her from year to year
when he works her with the breed that comes from horses. 340

The tribe of the lighthearted birds he snares
and takes prisoner the races of savage beasts
and the brood of the fish of the sea,
with the close-spun web of nets.
A cunning fellow is man. His contrivances
make him master of beasts of the field
and those that move in the mountains.
So he brings the horse with the shaggy neck   350
to bend underneath the yoke;
and also the untamed mountain bull;
and speech and windswift thought
and the tempers that go with city living
he has taught himself, and how to avoid
the sharp frost, when lodging is cold
under the open sky
and pelting strokes of the rain.
He has a way against everything,
and he faces nothing that is to come
without contrivance.   360
Only against death
can he call on no means of escape;
but escape from hopeless diseases

he has found in the depths of his mind.
With some sort of cunning, inventive
beyond all expectation
he reaches sometimes evil,
and sometimes good.

If he honors the laws of earth,
and the justice of the gods he has confirmed by oath,
high is his city; no city   370
has he with whom dwells dishonor
prompted by recklessness.
He who is so, may he never
share my hearth!
may he never think my thoughts!

Is this a portent sent by God?
I cannot tell.
I know her. How can I say
that this is not Antigone?
Unhappy girl, child of unhappy Oedipus,   380
what is this?
Surely it is not you they bring here
as disobedient to the royal edict,
surely not you, taken in such folly.

Sentry

She is the one who did the deed;
we took her burying him. But where is Creon?

Chorus

He is just coming from the house, when you most need him.

Creon

What is this? What has happened that I come
so opportunely?

Sentry

My lord, there is nothing
that a man should swear he would never do.

Second thoughts make liars of the first resolution.
I would have vowed it would be long enough   390
before I came again, lashed hence by your threats.
But since the joy that comes past hope, and against all hope,
is like no other pleasure in extent,
I have come here, though I break my oath in coming.
I bring this girl here who has been captured
giving the grace of burial to the dead man.
This time no lot chose me; this was my jackpot,
and no one else's. Now, my lord, take her
and as you please judge her and test her; I
am justly free and clear of all this trouble.   400

Creon
This girl—how did you take her and from where?

Sentry
She was burying the man. Now you know all.

Creon
Do you know what you are saying? Do you mean it?

Sentry
She is the one; I saw her burying
the dead man you forbade the burial of.
Now, do I speak plainly and clearly enough?

Creon
How was she seen? How was she caught in the act?

Sentry
This is how it was. When we came there,
with those dreadful threats of yours upon us,
we brushed off all the dust that lay upon
the dead man's body, heedfully
leaving it moist and naked.   410
We sat on the brow of the hill, to windward,
that we might shun the smell of the corpse upon us.

Each of us wakefully urged his fellow
with torrents of abuse, not to be careless
in this work of ours. So it went on,
until in the midst of the sky the sun's bright circle
stood still; the heat was burning. Suddenly
a squall lifted out of the earth a storm of dust,
a trouble in the sky. It filled the plain,
ruining all the foliage of the wood   420
that was around it. The great empty air
was filled with it. We closed our eyes, enduring
this plague sent by the gods. When at long last
we were quit of it, why, then we saw the girl.

She was crying out with the shrill cry
of an embittered bird
that sees its nest robbed of its nestlings
and the bed empty. So, too, when she saw
the body stripped of its cover, she burst out in groans,
calling terrible curses on those that had done that deed;
and with her hands immediately
brought thirsty dust to the body; from a shapely brazen   430
urn, held high over it, poured a triple stream
of funeral offerings; and crowned the corpse.
When we saw that, we rushed upon her and
caught our quarry then and there, not a bit disturbed.
We charged her with what she had done, then and the first time.
She did not deny a word of it—to my joy,
but to my pain as well. It is most pleasant
to have escaped oneself out of such troubles
but painful to bring into it those whom we love.
However, it is but natural for me
to count all this less than my own escape.   440

Creon
     You there, that turn your eyes upon the ground,
     do you confess or deny what you have done?

Antigone
> Yes, I confess; I will not deny my deed.

Creon (to the Sentry)
> You take yourself off where you like.
> You are free of a heavy charge.
> Now, Antigone, tell me shortly and to the point,
> did you know the proclamation against your action?

Antigone
> I knew it; of course I did. For it was public.

Creon
> And did you dare to disobey that law?

Antigone
> Yes, it was not Zeus that made the proclamation;   450
> nor did Justice, which lives with those below, enact
> such laws as that, for mankind. I did not believe
> your proclamation had such power to enable
> one who will someday die to override
> God's ordinances, unwritten and secure.
> *They* are not of today and yesterday;
> they live forever; none knows when first they were.
> These are the laws whose penalties I would not
> incur from the gods, through fear of any man's temper.
>
> I know that I will die—of course I do—   460
> even if you had not doomed me by proclamation.
> If I shall die before my time, I count that
> a profit. How can such as I, that live
> among such troubles, not find a profit in death?
> So for such as me, to face such a fate as this
> is pain that does not count. But if I dared to leave
> the dead man, my mother's son, dead and unburied,
> that would have been real pain. The other is not.
> Now, if you think me a fool to act like this,
> perhaps it is a fool that judges so.   470

Chorus

    The savage spirit of a savage father
    shows itself in this girl. She does not know
    how to yield to trouble.

Creon

    I would have you know the most fanatic spirits
    fall most of all. It is the toughest iron,
    baked in the fire to hardness, you may see
    most shattered, twisted, shivered to fragments.
    I know hot horses are restrained
    by a small curb. For he that is his neighbor's slave cannot
    be high in spirit. This girl had learned her insolence   480
    before this, when she broke the established laws.
    But here is still another insolence
    in that she boasts of it, laughs at what she did.
    I swear I am no man and she the man
    if she can win this and not pay for it.
    No; though she were my sister's child or closer
    in blood than all that my hearth god acknowledges
    as mine, neither she nor her sister should escape
    the utmost sentence—death. For indeed I accuse her,
    the sister, equally of plotting the burial.   490
    Summon her. I saw her inside, just now,
    crazy, distraught. When people plot
    mischief in the dark, it is the mind which first
    is convicted of deceit. But surely I hate indeed
    the one that is caught in evil and then makes
    that evil look like good.

Antigone

    Do you want anything
    beyond my taking and my execution?

Creon

    Oh, nothing! Once I have that I have everything.

Antigone

    Why do you wait, then? Nothing that you say
    pleases me; God forbid it ever should.   500
    So my words, too, naturally offend you.
    Yet how could I win a greater share of glory
    than putting my own brother in his grave?
    All that are here would surely say that's true,
    if fear did not lock their tongues up. A prince's power
    is blessed in many things, not least in this,
    that he can say and do whatever he likes.

Creon

    You are alone among the people of Thebes
    to see things in that way.

Antigone

    No, these do, too,
    but keep their mouths shut for the fear of you.

Creon

    Are you not ashamed to think so differently   510
    from them?

Antigone

    There is nothing shameful in honoring my brother.

Creon

    Was not he that died on the other side your brother?

Antigone

    Yes, indeed, of my own blood from father and mother.

Creon

    Why then do you show a grace that must be impious
    in *his* sight?

Antigone

    That other dead man
    would never bear you witness in what you say.

Creon

Yes he would, if you put him only on equality
with one that was a desecrator.

Antigone

It was his brother, not his slave, that died.

Creon

He died destroying the country the other defended.

Antigone

The god of death demands these rites for both.

Creon

But the good man does not seek an *equal* share only,   520
with the bad.

Antigone

Who knows
if in that other world this is true piety?

Creon

My enemy is still my enemy, even in death.

Antigone

My nature is to join in love, not hate.

Creon

Go then to the world below, yourself, if you
must love. Love *them*. When I am alive no woman shall rule.

Chorus

Here before the gates comes Ismene
shedding tears for the love of a brother.
A cloud over her brow casts shame
on her flushed face, as the tears wet
her fair cheeks.   530

Creon

You there, who lurked in my house, viper-like—
secretly drawing its lifeblood; I never thought

that I was raising two sources of destruction,
two rebels against my throne. Come tell me now,
will you, too, say you bore a hand in the burial
or will you swear that you know nothing of it?

Ismene

I did it, yes—if she will say I did it
I bear my share in it, bear the guilt, too.

Antigone

Justice will not allow you what you refused
and I will have none of your partnership.

Ismene

But in your troubles I am not ashamed   540
to sail with you the sea of suffering.

Antigone

Where the act was death, the dead are witnesses.
I do not love a friend who loves in words.

Ismene

Sister, do not dishonor me, denying me
a common death with you, a common honoring
of the dead man.

Antigone

Don't die with me, nor make your own
what you have never touched. I that die am enough.

Ismene

What life is there for me, once I have lost you?

Antigone

Ask Creon; all your care was on his behalf.

Ismene

Why do you hurt me, when you gain nothing by it?   550

Antigone

I am hurt by my own mockery—if I mock you.

Ismene

Even now—what can I do to help you still?

Antigone

Save yourself; I do not grudge you your escape.

Ismene

I cannot bear it! Not even to share your death!

Antigone

Life was your choice, and death was mine.

Ismene

You cannot say I accepted that choice in silence.

Antigone

You were right in the eyes of one party, I in the other.

Ismene

Well then, the fault is equally between us.

Antigone

Take heart; you are alive, but my life died
long ago, to serve the dead.   560

Creon

Here are two girls; I think that one of them
has suddenly lost her wits—the other was always so.

Ismene

Yes, for, my lord, the wits that they are born with
do not stay firm for the unfortunate.
They go astray.

Creon

Certainly yours do,
when you share troubles with the troublemaker.

Ismene

What life can be mine alone without her?

Creon

Do not
speak of *her*. *She* isn't, anymore.

Ismene
  Will you kill your son's wife to be?

Creon
  Yes, there are other fields for him to plough.

Ismene
  Not with the mutual love of him and her.   570

Creon
  I hate a bad wife for a son of mine.

Antigone
  Dear Haemon, how your father dishonors you.

Creon
  There is too much of you—and of your marriage!

Chorus
  Will you rob your son of this girl?

Creon
  Death—it is death that will stop the marriage for me.

Chorus
  Your decision it seems is taken: she shall die.

Creon
  Both you and I have decided it. No more delay.

                              (He turns to the servants.)

  Bring her inside, you. From this time forth,
  these must be women, and not free to roam.
  For even the stout of heart shrink when they see   580
  the approach of death close to their lives.

Chorus
              Lucky are those whose lives
              know no taste of sorrow.
              But for those whose house has been shaken by God
              there is never cessation of ruin;
              it steals on generation after generation

within a breed. Even as the swell
is driven over the dark deep
by the fierce Thracian winds   590
I see the ancient evils of Labdacus' house
are heaped on the evils of the dead.
No generation frees another, some god
strikes them down; there is no deliverance.
Here was the light of hope stretched
over the last roots of Oedipus' house,   600
and the bloody dust due to the gods below
has mowed it down—that and the folly of speech
and ruin's enchantment of the mind.

Your power, O Zeus, what sin of man can limit?
All-aging sleep does not overtake it,
nor the unwearied months of the gods; and you,
for whom times brings no age,
you hold the glowing brightness of Olympus.   610

For the future near and far,
and the past, this law holds good:
nothing very great
comes to the life of mortal man
without ruin to accompany it.
For Hope, widely wandering, comes to many of mankind
as a blessing,
but to many as the deceiver,
using light-minded lusts;
she comes to him that knows nothing
till he burns his foot in the glowing fire.
With wisdom has someone declared
a word of distinction: 620
that evil seems good to one whose mind
the god leads to ruin,
and but for the briefest moment of time
is his life outside of calamity.

Here is Haemon, youngest of your sons.
Does he come grieving
for the fate of his bride to be,
in agony at being cheated of his marriage?   630

Creon

Soon we will know that better than the prophets.
My son, can it be that you have not heard
of my final decision on your betrothed?
Can you have come here in your fury against your father?
Or have I your love still, no matter what I do?

Haemon

Father, I am yours; with your excellent judgment
you lay the right before me, and I shall follow it.
No marriage will ever be so valued by me
as to override the goodness of your leadership.

Creon

Yes, my son, this should always be
in your very heart, that everything else   640
shall be second to your father's decision.
It is for this that fathers pray to have
obedient sons begotten in their halls,
that they may requite with ill their father's enemy
and honor his friend no less than he would himself.
If a man have sons that are no use to him,
what can one say of him but that he has bred
so many sorrows to himself, laughter to his enemies?
Do not, my son, banish your good sense
through pleasure in a woman, since you know
that the embrace grows cold   650
when an evil woman shares your bed and home.
What greater wound can there be than a false friend?
No. Spit on her, throw her out like an enemy,
this girl, to marry someone in Death's house.
I caught her openly in disobedience
alone out of all this city and I shall not make

myself a liar in the city's sight. No, I will kill her.
So let her cry if she will on the Zeus of kinship;
for if I rear those of my race and breeding
to be rebels, surely I will do so with those outside it.   660
For he who is in his household a good man
will be found a just man, too, in the city.
But he that breaches the law or does it violence
or thinks to dictate to those who govern him
shall never have my good word.
The man the city sets up in authority
must be obeyed in small things and in just
but also in their opposites.
I am confident such a man of whom I speak
will be a good ruler, and willing to be well ruled.
He will stand on his country's side, faithful and just,   670
in the storm of battle. There is nothing worse
than disobedience to authority.
It destroys cities, it demolishes homes;
it breaks and routs one's allies. Of successful lives
the most of them are saved by discipline.
So we must stand on the side of what is orderly;
we cannot give victory to a woman.
If we must accept defeat, let it be from a man;
we must not let people say that a woman beat us.   680

Chorus

We think, if we are not victims of Time the Thief,
that you speak intelligently of what you speak.

Haemon

Father, the natural sense that the gods breed
in men is surely the best of their possessions.
I certainly could not declare you wrong—
may I never know how to do so!—Still there might
be something useful that some other than you might think.
It is natural for me to be watchful on your behalf
concerning what all men say or do or find to blame.

Your face is terrible to a simple citizen;   690
it frightens him from words you dislike to hear.
But what *I* can hear, in the dark, are things like these:
the city mourns for this girl; they think she is dying
most wrongly and most undeservedly
of all womenkind, for the most glorious acts.
Here is one who would not leave her brother unburied,
a brother who had fallen in bloody conflict,
to meet his end by greedy dogs or by
the bird that chanced that way. Surely what she merits
is golden honor, isn't it? That's the dark rumor
that spreads in secret. Nothing I own   700
I value more highly, father, than your success.
What greater distinction can a son have than the glory
of a successful father, and for a father
the distinction of successful children?
Do not bear this single habit of mind, to think
that what you say and nothing else is true.
A man who thinks that he alone is right,
or what he says, or what he *is* himself,
unique, such men, when opened up, are seen
to be quite empty. For a man, though he be wise,   710
it is no shame to learn—learn many things,
and not maintain his views too rigidly.
You notice how by streams in wintertime
the trees that yield preserve their branches safely,
but those that fight the tempest perish utterly.
The man who keeps the sheet of his sail tight
and never slackens capsizes his boat
and makes the rest of his trip keel uppermost.
Yield something of your anger, give way a little.
If a much younger man, like me, may have
a judgment, I would say it were far better   720
to be one altogether wise by nature, but,
as things incline not to be so, then it is good
also to learn from those who advise well.

Chorus
  My lord, if he says anything to the point,
  you should learn from him, and you, too, Haemon,
  learn from your father. Both of you
  have spoken well.

Creon
  Should we that are my age learn wisdom
  from young men such as he is?

Haemon
  Not learn injustice, certainly. If I am young,
  do not look at my years but what I do.

Creon
  Is what you do to have respect for rebels?   730

Haemon
                                    I
  would not urge you to be scrupulous
  towards the wicked.

Creon
  Is *she* not tainted by the disease of wickedness?

Haemon
  The entire people of Thebes says no to that.

Creon
  Should the city tell me how I am to rule them?

Haemon
  Do you see what a young man's words these are of yours?

Creon
  Must I rule the land by someone else's judgment
  rather than my own?

Haemon
                      There is no city
  possessed by one man only.

Creon
  Is not the city thought to be the ruler's?

Haemon

You would be a fine dictator of a desert.

Creon

It seems this boy is on the woman's side. 740

Haemon

If you are a woman—my care is all for you.

Creon

You villain, to bandy words with your own father!

Haemon

I see your acts as mistaken and unjust.

Creon

Am I mistaken, reverencing my own office?

Haemon

There is no reverence in trampling on God's honor.

Creon

Your nature is vile, in yielding to a woman.

Haemon

You will not find me yield to what is shameful.

Creon

At least, your argument is all for her.

Haemon

Yes, and for you and me—and for the gods below.

Creon

You will never marry her while her life lasts. 750

Haemon

Then she must die—and dying destroy another.

Creon

Has your daring gone so far, to threaten me?

Haemon

What threat is it to speak against empty judgments?

Creon

> Empty of sense yourself, you will regret
> your schooling of me in sense.

Haemon

>   If you were not
> my father, I would say you are insane.

Creon

> You woman's slave, do not try to wheedle me.

Haemon

> You want to talk but never to hear and listen.

Creon

> Is that so? By the heavens above you will not—
> be sure of that—get off scot-free, insulting,
> abusing me.

>   (He speaks to the servants.)

>   You people bring out this creature,
> this hated creature, that she may die before   760
> his very eyes, right now, next her would-be husband.

Haemon

> Not at my side! Never think that! She will not
> die by my side. But you will never again
> set eyes upon my face. Go then and rage
> with such of your friends as are willing to endure it.

Chorus

> The man is gone, my lord, quick in his anger.
> A young man's mind is fierce when he is hurt.

Creon

> Let him go, and do and think things superhuman.
> But these two girls he shall not save from death.

Chorus

> Both of them? Do you mean to kill them both?   770

Creon

   No, not the one that didn't do anything.
   You are quite right there.

Chorus

   And by what form of death do you mean to kill her?

Creon

   I will bring her where the path is loneliest,
   and hide her alive in a rocky cavern there.
   I'll give just enough of food as shall suffice
   for a bare expiation, that the city may avoid pollution.
   In that place she shall call on Hades, god of death,
   in her prayers. That god only she reveres.
   Perhaps she will win from him escape from death
   or at least in that last moment will recognize
   her honoring of the dead is labor lost.   780

Chorus

          Love undefeated in the fight,
          Love that makes havoc of possessions,
          Love who lives at night in a young girl's soft cheeks,
          Who travels over sea, or in huts in the countryside—
          there is no god able to escape you
          nor anyone of men, whose life is a day only,
          and whom you possess is mad.   790

          You wrench the minds of just men to injustice,
          to their disgrace; this conflict among kinsmen
          it is you who stirred to turmoil.
          The winner is desire. She gleaming kindles
          from the eyes of the girl good to bed.
          Love shares the throne with the great powers that rule.
          For the golden Aphrodite holds her play there
          and then no one can overcome her.   800

          Here I too am borne out of the course of lawfulness
          when I see these things, and I cannot control
          the springs of my tears

when I see Antigone making her way
to her bed—but the bed
that is rest for everyone.

Antigone

You see me, you people of my country,
as I set out on my last road of all,
looking for the last time on this light of this sun—
never again. I am alive but Hades who gives sleep to everyone
is leading me to the shores of Acheron,   810
though I have known nothing of marriage songs
nor the chant that brings the bride to bed.
My husband is to be the Lord of Death.

Chorus

Yes, you go to the place where the dead are hidden,
but you go with distinction and praise.
You have not been stricken by wasting sickness;
you have not earned the wages of the sword;   820
it was your own choice and alone among mankind
you will descend, alive,
to that world of death.

Antigone

But indeed I have heard of the saddest of deaths—
of the Phrygian stranger, daughter of Tantalus,
whom the rocky growth subdued, like clinging ivy.
The rains never leave her, the snow never fails,
as she wastes away. That is how men tell the story.
From streaming eyes her tears wet the crags;   830
most like to her the god brings me to rest.

Chorus

Yes, but she was a god, and god born,
and you are mortal and mortal born.
Surely it is great renown
for a woman that dies, that in life and death
her lot is a lot shared with demigods.

Antigone

You mock me. In the name of our fathers' gods
why do you not wait till I am gone to insult me?   840
Must you do it face to face?
My city! Rich citizens of my city!
You springs of Dirce, you holy groves of Thebes,
famed for its chariots! I would still have you as my witnesses,
with what dry-eyed friends, under what laws
I make my way to my prison sealed like a tomb.
Pity me. Neither among the living nor the dead   850
do I have a home in common—
neither with the living nor the dead.

Chorus

You went to the extreme of daring
and against the high throne of Justice
you fell, my daughter, grievously.
But perhaps it was for some ordeal of your father
that you are paying requital.

Antigone

You have touched the most painful of my cares—
the pity for my father, ever reawakened,
and the fate of all of our race, the famous Labdacids;   860
the doomed self-destruction of my mother's bed
when she slept with her own son,
my father.
What parents I was born of, God help me!
To them I am going to share their home,
the curse on me, too, and unmarried.
Brother, it was a luckless marriage you made,   870
and dying killed my life.

Chorus

There *is* a certain reverence for piety.
But for him in authority,
he cannot see that authority defied;

it is your own self-willed temper
that has destroyed you.

Antigone

No tears for me, no friends, no marriage. Brokenhearted
I am led along the road ready before me.
I shall never again be suffered
to look on the holy eye of the day.   880
But my fate claims no tears—
no friend cries for me.

Creon (to the servants)

Don't you know that weeping and wailing before death
would never stop if one is allowed to weep and wail?
Lead her away at once. Enfold her
in that rocky tomb of hers—as I told you to.
There leave her alone, solitary,
to die if she so wishes
or live a buried life in such a home;
we are guiltless in respect of her, this girl.
But living above, among the rest of us, this life
she shall certainly lose.   890

Antigone

Tomb, bridal chamber, prison forever
dug in rock, it is to you I am going
to join my people, that great number that have died,
whom in their death Persephone received.
I am the last of them and I go down
in the worst death of all—for I have not lived
the due term of my life. But when I come
to that other world my hope is strong
that my coming will be welcome to my father,
and dear to you, my mother, and dear to you,
my brother deeply loved. For when you died,   900
with my own hands I washed and dressed you all,
and poured the lustral offerings on your graves.

And now, Polyneices, it was for such care of your body
that I have earned these wages.
Yet those who think rightly will think I did right
in honoring you. Had I been a mother
of children, and my husband been dead and rotten,
I would not have taken this weary task upon me
against the will of the city. What law backs me
when I say this? I will tell you:
If my husband were dead, I might have had another,
and child from another man, if I lost the first.   910
But when father and mother both were hidden in death
no brother's life would bloom for me again.
That is the law under which I gave you precedence,
my dearest brother, and that is why Creon thinks me
wrong, even a criminal, and now takes me
by the hand and leads me away,
unbedded, without bridal, without share
in marriage and in nurturing of children;
as lonely as you see me; without friends;
with fate against me I go to the vault of death   920
while still alive. What law of God have I broken?
Why should I still look to the gods in my misery?
Whom should I summon as ally? For indeed
because of piety I was called impious.
If this proceeding is good in the gods' eyes
I shall know my sin, once I have suffered.
But if Creon and his people are the wrongdoers
let their suffering be no worse than the injustice
they are meting out to me.

Chorus

It is the same blasts, the tempests of the soul,
possess her.   930

Creon

                    Then for this her guards,
who are so slow, will find themselves in trouble.

Antigone (cries out)
 Oh, that word has come
 very close to death.

Creon
 I will not comfort you
 with hope that the sentence will not be accomplished.

Antigone
 O my father's city, in Theban land,
 O gods that sired my race,
 I am led away, I have no more stay.
 Look on me, princes of Thebes,   940
 the last remnant of the old royal line;
 see what I suffer and who makes me suffer
 because I gave reverence to what claims reverence.

Chorus
    Danae suffered, too, when, her beauty lost, she gave
    the light of heaven in exchange for brassbound walls,
    and in the tomb-like cell was she hidden and held;
    yet she was honored in her breeding, child,
    and she kept, as guardian, the seed of Zeus
    that came to her in a golden shower.   950
    But there is some terrible power in destiny
    and neither wealth nor war
    nor tower nor black ships, beaten by the sea,
    can give escape from it.

    The hot-tempered son of Dryas, the Edonian king,
    in fury mocked Dionysus,
    who then held him in restraint
    in a rocky dungeon.
    So the terrible force and flower of his madness   960
    drained away. He came to know the god
    whom in frenzy he had touched with his mocking tongue,
    when he would have checked the inspired women
    and the fire of Dionysus,
    when he provoked the Muses that love the lyre.

By the black rocks, dividing the sea in two,
are the shores of the Bosporus, Thracian Salmydessus.   970
There the god of war who lives near the city
saw the terrible blinding wound
dealt by his savage wife
on Phineus' two sons.
She blinded and tore with the points of her shuttle,
and her bloodied hands, those eyes
that else would have looked on her vengefully.
As they wasted away, they lamented
their unhappy fate that they were doomed
to be born of a mother cursed in her marriage.   980
She traced her descent from the seed
of the ancient Erechtheidae.
In far-distant caves she was raised
among her father's storms, that child of Boreas,
quick as a horse, over the steep hills,
a daughter of the gods.
But, my child, the long-lived Fates
bore hard upon her, too.

(Enter Teiresias, the blind prophet, led by a boy.)

Teiresias

My lords of Thebes, we have come here together,
one pair of eyes serving us both. For the blind
such must be the way of going, by a guide's leading.   990

Creon

What is the news, my old Teiresias?

Teiresias

I will tell you; and you, listen to the prophet.

Creon

Never in the past have I turned from your advice.

Teiresias

And so you have steered well the ship of state.

Creon

I have benefited and can testify to that.

Teiresias

Then realize you are on the razor edge
of danger.

Creon

What can that be? I shudder to hear those words.

Teiresias

When you learn the signs recognized by my art
you will understand.
I sat at my ancient place of divination   1000
for watching the birds, where every bird finds shelter;
and I heard an unwonted voice among them;
they were horribly distressed, and screamed unmeaningly.
I knew they were tearing each other murderously;
the beating of their wings was a clear sign.
I was full of fear; at once on all the altars,
as they were fully kindled, I tasted the offerings,
but the god of fire refused to burn from the sacrifice,
and from the thighbones a dark stream of moisture
oozed from the embers, smoked and sputtered.
The gall bladder burst and scattered to the air
and the streaming thighbones lay exposed   1010
from the fat wrapped round them—
so much I learned from this boy here,
the fading prophecies of a rite that failed.
This boy here is my guide, as I am others'.
This is the city's sickness—and your plans are the cause of it.
For our altars and our sacrificial hearths
are filled with the carrion meat of birds and dogs,
torn from the flesh of Oedipus' poor son.
So the gods will not take our prayers or sacrifice   1020
nor yet the flame from the thighbones, and no bird
cries shrill and clear, so glutted
are they with fat of the blood of the killed man.

Reflect on these things, son. All men
can make mistakes; but, once mistaken,
a man is no longer stupid nor accursed
who, having fallen on ill, tries to cure that ill,
not taking a fine undeviating stand.
It is obstinacy that convicts of folly.
Yield to the dead man; do not stab him—
now he is gone—what bravery is this,
to inflict another death upon the dead?   1030
I mean you well and speak well for your good.
It is never sweeter to learn from a good counselor
than when he counsels to your benefit.

Creon

Old man, you are all archers, and I am your mark.
I must be tried by your prophecies as well.
By the breed of you I have been bought and sold
and made a merchandise, for ages now.
But I tell you: make your profit from silver-gold
from Sardis and the gold from India
if you will. But this dead man you shall not hide
in a grave, not though the eagles of Zeus should bear   1040
the carrion, snatching it to the throne of Zeus itself.
Even so, I shall not so tremble at the pollution
to let you bury him.

          No, I am certain
no human has the power to pollute the gods.
They fall, you old Teiresias, those men,
—so very clever—in a bad fall whenever
they eloquently speak vile words for profit.

Teiresias

I wonder if there's a man who dares consider—

Creon

What do you mean? What sort of generalization
is this talk of yours?

Teiresias

How much the best of possessions is the ability   1050
to listen to wise advice?

Creon

As I should imagine that the worst
injury must be native stupidity.

Teiresias

Now that is exactly where your mind is sick.

Creon

I do not like to answer a seer with insults.

Teiresias

But you do, when you say my prophecies are lies.

Creon

Well,
the whole breed of prophets certainly loves money.

Teiresias

And the breed that comes from princes loves to take
advantage—base advantage.

Creon

Do you realize
you are speaking in such terms of your own prince?

Teiresias

I know. But it is through me you have saved the city.

Creon

You are a wise prophet, but what you love is wrong.

Teiresias

You will force me to declare what should be hidden   1060
in my own heart.

Creon

Out with it—
but only if your words are not for gain.

Teiresias

They won't be for *your* gain—that I am sure of.

Creon

But realize you will not make a merchandise
of my decisions.

Teiresias

And you must realize
that you will not outlive many cycles more
of this swift sun before you give in exchange
one of your own loins bred, a corpse for a corpse,
for you have thrust one that belongs above
below the earth, and bitterly dishonored
a living soul by lodging her in the grave;
while one that belonged indeed to the underworld
gods you have kept on this earth without due share   1070
of rites of burial, of due funeral offerings,
a corpse unhallowed. With all of this you, Creon,
have nothing to do, nor have the gods above.
These acts of yours are violence, on your part.
And in requital the avenging Spirits
of Death itself and the gods' Furies shall
after *your* deeds, lie in ambush for you, and
in their hands you shall be taken cruelly.
Now, look at this and tell me I was bribed
to say it! The delay will not be long
before the cries of mourning in your house,
of men and women. All the cities will stir in hatred   1080
against you, because their sons in mangled shreds
received their burial rites from dogs, from wild beasts
or when some bird of the air brought a vile stink
to each city that contained the hearths of the dead.
These are the arrows that archer-like I launched—
you vexed me so to anger—at your heart.
You shall not escape their sting. You, boy,

lead me away to my house, so he may discharge
his anger on younger men; so may he come to know
to bear a quieter tongue in his head and a better
mind than that now he carries in him.   1090

Chorus

That was a terrible prophecy, my lord.
The man has gone. Since these hairs of mine grew white
from the black they once were, he has never spoken
a word of a lie to our city.

Creon

I know, I know.
My mind is all bewildered. To yield is terrible.
But by opposition to destroy my very being
with a self-destructive curse must also be reckoned
in what is terrible.

Chorus

You need good counsel, son of Menoeceus,
and need to take it.

Creon

What must I do, then? Tell me; I shall agree.

Chorus

The girl—go now and bring her up from her cave,   1100
and for the exposed dead man, give him his burial.

Creon

That is really your advice? You would have me yield.

Chorus

And quickly as you may, my lord. Swift harms
sent by the gods cut off the paths of the foolish.

Creon

Oh, it is hard; I must give up what my heart
would have me do. But it is ill to fight
against what must be.

Chorus

> Go now, and do this;
> do not give the task to others.

Creon

> I will go,
> just as I am. Come, servants, all of you;
> take axes in your hands; away with you
> to the place you see, there. 1110
> For my part, since my intention is so changed,
> as I bound her myself, myself will free her.
> I am afraid it may be best, in the end
> of life, to have kept the old accepted laws.

Chorus

> You of many names, glory of the Cadmeian
> bride, breed of loud thundering Zeus;
> you who watch over famous Italy;
> you who rule where all are welcome in Eleusis;
> in the sheltered plains of Deo—
> O Bacchus that dwells in Thebes, 1120
> the mother city of Bacchanals,
> by the flowing stream of Ismenus,
> in the ground sown by the fierce dragon's teeth.
>
> You are he on whom the murky gleam of torches glares,
> above the twin peaks of the crag
> where come the Corycean nymphs
> to worship you, the Bacchanals;
> and the stream of Castalia has seen you, too; 1130
> and you are he that the ivy-clad
> slopes of Nisaean hills,
> and the green shore ivy-clustered,
> sent to watch over the roads of Thebes,
> where the immortal Evoe chant rings out.
>
> It is Thebes which you honor most of all cities,
> you and your mother both,
> she who died by the blast of Zeus' thunderbolt.

And now when the city, with all its folk,   1140
is gripped by a violent plague,
come with healing foot, over the slopes of Parnassus,
over the moaning strait.
You lead the dance of the fire-breathing stars,
you are master of the voices of the night.
True-born child of Zeus, appear,
my lord, with your Thyiad attendants,
who in frenzy all night long
dance in your house, Iacchus,   1150
dispenser of gifts.

Messenger

You who live by the house of Cadmus and Amphion,
hear me. There is no condition of man's life
that stands secure. As such I would not
praise it or blame. It is chance that sets upright;
it is chance that brings down the lucky and the unlucky,
each in his turn. For men, that belong to death,
there is no prophet of established things.   1160
Once Creon was a man worthy of envy—
of my envy, at least. For he saved this city
of Thebes from her enemies, and attained
the throne of the land, with all a king's power.
He guided it right. His race bloomed
with good children. But when a man forfeits joy
I do not count his life as life, but only
a life trapped in a corpse.
Be rich within your house, yes greatly rich,
if so you will, and live in a prince's style.
If the gladness of these things is gone, I would not   1170
give the shadow of smoke for the rest,
as against joy.

Chorus

What is the sorrow of our princes
of which you are the messenger?

Messenger

Death; and the living are guilty of their deaths.

Chorus

But who is the murderer? Who the murdered? Tell us.

Messenger

Haemon is dead; the hand that shed his blood
was his very own.

Chorus

Truly his own hand? Or his father's?

Messenger

His own hand, in his anger
against his father for a murder.

Chorus

Prophet, how truly you have made good your word!

Messenger

These things are so; you may debate the rest.

Chorus

Here I see Creon's wife Eurydice   1180
approaching. Unhappy woman!
Does she come from the house as hearing about her son
or has she come by chance?

Eurydice

I heard your words, all you men of Thebes, as I
was going out to greet Pallas with my prayers.
I was just drawing back the bolts of the gate
to open it when a cry struck through my ears
telling of my household's ruin. I fell backward
in terror into the arms of my servants; I fainted.
But tell me again, what is the story? I   1190
will hear it as one who is no stranger to sorrow.

Messenger

Dear mistress, I will tell you, for I was there,
and I will leave out no word of the truth.

Why should I comfort you and then tomorrow
be proved a liar? The truth is always best.

I followed your husband, at his heels, to the end of the plain
where Polyneices' body still lay unpitied,
and torn by dogs. We prayed to Hecate, goddess
of the crossroads, and also to Pluto   1200
that they might restrain their anger and turn kind.
And him we washed with sacred lustral water
and with fresh-cut boughs we burned what was left of him
and raised a high mound of his native earth;
then we set out again for the hollowed rock,
death's stone bridal chamber for the girl.
Someone then heard a voice of bitter weeping
while we were still far off, coming from that unblest room.
The man came to tell our master Creon of it.
As the king drew nearer, there swarmed about him
a cry of misery but no clear words.
He groaned and in an anguished mourning voice   1210
cried "Oh, am I a true prophet? Is this the road
that I must travel, saddest of all my wayfaring?
It is my son's voice that haunts my ear. Servants,
get closer, quickly. Stand around the tomb
and look. There is a gap there where the stones
have been wrenched away; enter there, by the very mouth,
and see whether I recognize the voice of Haemon
or if the gods deceive me." On the command
of our despairing master we went to look.
In the furthest part of the tomb we saw her, hanging   1220
by her neck. She had tied a noose of muslin on it.
Haemon's hands were about her waist embracing her,
while he cried for the loss of his bride gone to the dead,
and for all his father had done, and his own sad love.
When Creon saw him he gave a bitter cry,
went in and called to him with a groan: "Poor son!
what have you done? What can you have meant?

What happened to destroy you? Come out, I pray you!"   1230
The boy glared at him with savage eyes, and then
spat in his face, without a word of answer.
He drew his double-hilted sword. As his father
ran to escape him, Haemon failed to strike him,
and the poor wretch in anger at himself
leaned on his sword and drove it halfway in,
into his ribs. Then he folded the girl to him,
in his arms, while he was conscious still,
and gasping poured a sharp stream of bloody drops
on her white cheeks. There they lie,
the dead upon the dead. So he has won   1240
the pitiful fulfillment of his marriage
within death's house. In this human world he has shown
how the wrong choice in plans is for a man
his greatest evil.

Chorus

What do you make of this? My lady is gone,
without a word of good or bad.

Messenger

                I, too,
am lost in wonder. I am inclined to hope
that hearing of her son's death she could not
open her sorrow to the city, but chose rather
within her house to lay upon her maids
the mourning for the household grief. Her judgment
is good; she will not make any false step.   1250

Chorus

I do not know. To me this over-heavy silence
seems just as dangerous as much empty wailing.

Messenger

I will go in and learn if in her passionate
heart she keeps hidden some secret purpose.
You are right; there is sometimes danger in too much silence.

Chorus

> Here comes our king himself. He bears in his hands
> a memorial all too clear;
> it is a ruin of none other's making,
> purely his own if one dare to say that.   1260

Creon

> The mistakes of a blinded man
> are themselves rigid and laden with death.
> You look at us the killer and the killed
> of the one blood. Oh, the awful blindness
> of those plans of mine. My son, you were so young,
> so young to die. You were freed from the bonds of life
> through no folly of your own—only through mine.

Chorus

> I think you have learned justice—but too late.   1270

Creon

> Yes, I have learned it to my bitterness. At this moment
> God has sprung on my head with a vast weight
> and struck me down. He shook me in my savage ways;
> he has overturned my joy, has trampled it,
> underfoot. The pains men suffer
> are pains indeed.

Second Messenger

> My lord, you have troubles and a store besides;
> some are there in your hands, but there are others
> you will surely see when you come to your house.   1280

Creon

> What trouble can there be beside these troubles?

Second Messenger

> The queen is dead. She was indeed true mother
> of the dead son. She died, poor lady,
> by recent violence upon herself.

Creon

Haven of death, you can never have enough.
Why, why do you destroy me?
You messenger, who have brought me bitter news,
what is this tale you tell?
It is a dead man that you kill again—
what new message of yours is this, boy?
Is this new slaughter of a woman   1290
a doom to lie on the pile of the dead?

Chorus

You can see. It is no longer
hidden in a corner.

*(By some stage device, perhaps the so-called eccyclema, the inside of
the palace is shown, with the body of the dead Queen.)*

Creon

Here is yet another horror
for my unhappy eyes to see.
What doom still waits for me?
I have but now taken in my arms my son,
and again I look upon another dead face.
Poor mother and poor son!   1300

Second Messenger

She stood at the altar, and with keen whetted knife
she suffered her darkening eyes to close.
First she cried in agony recalling the noble fate of Megareus,
who died before all this,
and then for the fate of this son; and in the end
she cursed you for the evil you had done
in killing her sons.

Creon

I am distracted with fear. Why does not someone
strike a two-edged sword right through me?   1310
I am dissolved in an agony of misery.

Second Messenger

You were indeed accused
by her that is dead
of Haemon's and of Megareus' death.

Creon

By what kind of violence did she find her end?

Second Messenger

Her own hand struck her to the entrails
when she heard of her son's lamentable death.

Creon

These acts can never be made to fit another
to free me from the guilt. It was I that killed her.
Poor wretch that I am, I say it is true!
Servants, lead me away, quickly, quickly.
I am no more a live man than one dead.

1320

Chorus

What you say is for the best—if there be a best
in evil such as this. For the shortest way
is best with troubles that lie at our feet.

Creon

O, let it come, let it come,
that best of fates that waits on my last day.
Surely best fate of all. Let it come, let it come!
That I may never see one more day's light!

1330

Chorus

These things are for the future. We must deal
with what impends. What in the future is to care for
rests with those whose duty it is
to care for them.

Creon

At least, all that *I* want
is in that prayer of mine.

Chorus

    Pray for no more at all. For what is destined
    for us, men mortal, there is no escape.

Creon

    Lead me away, a vain silly man
    who killed you, son, and you, too, lady.   1340
    I did not mean to, but I did.
    I do not know where to turn my eyes
    to look to, for support.
    Everything in my hands is crossed. A most unwelcome fate
    has leaped upon me.

Chorus

    Wisdom is far the chief element in happiness
    and, secondly, no irreverence towards the gods.
    But great words of haughty men exact   1350
    in retribution blows as great
    and in old age teach wisdom.

THE COMPLETE GREEK TRAGEDIES

AESCHYLUS · I *ORESTEIA*

Translated and with an Introduction by Richmond Lattimore

Agamemnon
The Libation Bearers
The Eumenides

AESCHYLUS · II *FOUR TRAGEDIES*

The Suppliant Maidens. *S. G. Benardete*
The Persians. *S. G. Benardete*
Seven against Thebes. *David Grene*
Prometheus Bound. *David Grene*

SOPHOCLES · I *THREE TRAGEDIES*

Translated and with an Introduction by David Grene

Oedipus the King
Oedipus at Colonus
Antigone

SOPHOCLES · II *FOUR TRAGEDIES*

Ajax. *John Moore*
The Women of Trachis. *Michael Jameson*
Electra *and* Philoctetes. *David Grene*

EURIPIDES · I *FOUR TRAGEDIES*

With an Introduction by Richmond Lattimore

Alcestis. *Richmond Lattimore*
The Medea. *Rex Warner*
The Heracleidae. *Ralph Gladstone*
Hippolytus. *David Grene*

EURIPIDES · II *FOUR TRAGEDIES*

The Cyclops *and* Heracles. *William Arrowsmith*
Iphigenia in Tauris. *Witter Bynner. Introduction by Richmond Lattimore*
Helen. *Richmond Lattimore*

EURIPIDES · III *FOUR TRAGEDIES*

Hecuba. *William Arrowsmith*
Andromache. *John Frederick Nims*
The Trojan Women. *Richmond Lattimore*
Ion. *R. F. Willetts*

EURIPIDES · IV *FOUR TRAGEDIES*

Rhesus. *Richmond Lattimore*
The Suppliant Women. *Frank William Jones*
Orestes. *William Arrowsmith*
Iphigenia in Aulis. *Charles R. Walker*

EURIPIDES · V *THREE TRAGEDIES*

Electra. *Emily Townsend Vermeule*
The Phoenician Women. *Elizabeth Wyckoff*
The Bacchae. *William Arrowsmith*